Woodcarving
An introduction

Maurice Woods

D1335796

A & C Black · London

First published 1981
Reissued in paperback 1986
Reprinted 1987
A & C Black (Publishers) Ltd
35 Bedford Row, London WC1R 4JH

© 1981 Maurice Woods

ISBN 0–7136–2807–3

Woods, Maurice
Woodcarving.
1. Wood-carving – Techniques
I. Title
731.4'62   NK9704
ISBN 0–7136–2807–3

The photographs on pp. 38 and 69
are reproduced by courtesy of the
Victoria and Albert Museum.
Those on p. 50 are reproduced by
courtesy of the Trustees of the
British Museum. Many thanks to
Chris Hoggett for permission to
reproduce photographs from
Design with Scrap and to Peter
Etheredge for the use of
photographs of his carvings.

Filmset by August Filmsetting,
Stockport, Cheshire. Printed in
Great Britain at
The Bath Press, Avon

Contents

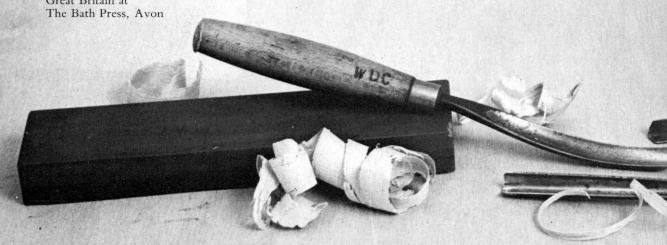

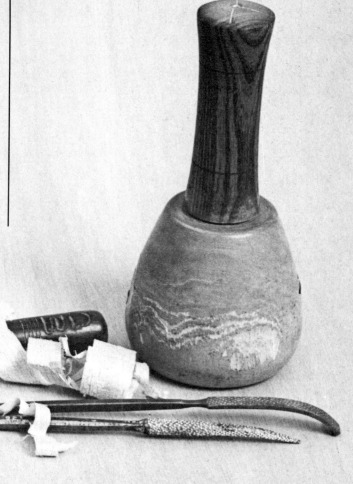

Timber reference

The woods described here are all suitable for carving and widely available in the U.K.

European timber

Ash	Grainy hardwood, pale yellow colouring.
Beech	Very hard, close-grained, light brown colouring.
Birch	Fairly hard, fine texture, pale yellow colouring.
Chestnut	Medium hardwood, pale yellow colouring.
Elm	Interesting grain, moderately hard, yellow/brown colouring.
Lime	Excellent to carve, low to moderate hardness, white/pale yellow colouring.
Oak	Tough, inconsistent grain texture, light brown colouring.
Plane	Good texture and workability, fairly hard, red/brown colouring.
Sycamore	Very hard compact texture, white/pale yellow colouring.
Walnut	A fancy hardwood, medium workability, rich variegated colouring.

West African timber

Makore	Medium hardwood, good texture, fair workability, red/brown colouring.
Sapele	Interlocked grain, moderate workability, red colouring.
Utile	Good workability, excellent texture, red/brown colouring.

East African timber

Olive	Fair workability, medium hardness, interesting grain figuration, light brown colouring.

North American timber

Maple (Rock)	Fine texture, good workability, white/pale yellow colouring.
Yellow pine	Moderate texture, easy workability, light brown colouring.

Introduction

Woodcarving may truly be described as an international craft. Timber, tools and technique may vary from one latitude to another, but the desire to create pleasing shapes from wood arises wherever trees are found. In spite of the popularity of carving, however, newcomers to the craft do not find either a great deal of practical instruction about it, or discriminating direction on what subjects are most suitable to carve. Beginners often have to start out on their own without really knowing what is within their capabilities.

Short of an instructor actually standing behind the beginner's elbow, the next best thing is a carefully planned course of written instruction, and I hope that this book will provide both guidance and companionship for the beginner on his way to becoming a competent carver.

It is not complicated to start woodcarving. From the outset I have assumed that the reader does not possess comprehensive workshop facilities or unlimited spending money. Lack of either commodity will not stop anyone from becoming a woodcarver. But a progressive approach to every aspect of the craft is absolutely essential and the successful completion of any model depends largely on the preliminary spade work.

I have explained the various stages of models with photographs and drawings, and I have included some finished work of my own and some by other carvers, past and present, to illustrate further the points I make. I should mention that work of a purely abstract nature is not discussed for, quite simply, I am unable to teach what I cannot understand. Again, the reader will find items for displaying around the home but no information on how to carve furniture, though light decorative cabinet chipping is covered.

Happily, the size of a model by no means determines the amount of pleasure and knowledge which may be acquired through working on it, and I have ensured that all the projects are a practical proposition from a physical and financial standpoint, and easily obtainable wood may be used to make them. No doubt some readers will be attracted to one particular type of carving, while others may have a preference for other subjects; perhaps nothing less than a combination of both will prove satisfactory.

The different aspects of the craft of carving are interesting. Time was when I considered the technique of letter cutting to be of little significance. With so many exciting things to make, why waste time on mundane letters? The moment I started earning my living with a chisel, it seemed as if the world was beating a path to my workshop door – all with letter cutting jobs. I appreciate that the average reader will be carving strictly for the enjoyable relaxation it offers, yet nevertheless every avenue of the craft is worthy of serious exploration before the decision is made to linger in any.

Wood sculpture is a close relative of woodcarving and it is rather difficult to make distinctions between them; I think the fairest way of defining wood sculpture is to say that it has no objective other than to please or intrigue the beholder. To this end the sculptor may exploit the beauty of the wood to its best advantage by creating a purely abstract shape. My own brief excursions into the world of fantasy are usually inspired by a tree branch of curious malformation. Often a little judicious adjustment will result in a shape bristling with neoteric vibrations.

Depending on the nature of the work, however, a happy compromise integrating old and new techniques is sometimes possible. I dislike using the word 'traditional' in connection with carving, for it conjures up a vision of dust-trapping configurations which are a silent testimony to an era of superhuman patience. (There is, of course, no denying that the carvers of yesteryear were masters of their medium.) But for me, contemporary carving will possess modern smoothness with a traditional flavour – I prefer to come to terms with wood by eliminating any features of a subject that look hostile to the material. Let's take it from there.

Workshop safety

When your concentration is wholly on your work, you are not fully prepared for unexpected dangers. Providing a few sensible precautions are taken, however, the unexpected should never happen. The carver's first responsibility is to himself, and safety should always come first.

It is important that you consider carefully the best way to secure a carving while you are working on it; if you choose to grip a model lightly in a vice (even if you think that ordinary working pressure may damage it) you do run the risk of real injury to yourself.

Sharp cutting tools are dangerous and need to be treated with respect. Always keep both hands safely behind the cutting direction of a chisel. Remember too that these tools are prone to roll off the bench top, and damage both their fragile tips and carvers' feet. A cluttered bench top does not make for safe working – get into the habit of replacing every tool as you work. Hand sawing and planing wood requires both adequate elbow room and a firm foundation. Neither tool must be used over-energetically; too much force may result in the sudden parting of an off-cut, or irretrievable loss of balance if the workpiece slips while planing.

The potential hazards of small machine tools are rarely recognised until accidents occur, and these nearly always happen because of carelessness. Never leave a portable machine connected at its power source, and always make sure that a machine switch is in the 'off' position before plugging it in. Never remove a machine guard, even if it does seem more convenient to operate the machine without it. Holding the workpiece while using a fine drill may prove painful if the drill breaks; the stump remaining in the machine may plunge downwards into an unsuspecting finger. When an electric drill is used to spin a grinding wheel, eye protection is essential. Always ensure that the work is securely held when using a machine tool, as the vibrations will tend to slacken the grip.

The quality of light is very important in a workshop. You are tempting fate if you work in a garden shed with a small window as your only source of light. Fitting a fanlight over the bench gives a fairly constant and effective light source. Electric light is not particularly suitable for carving purposes, but it is better than no light at all during the winter months. A flexible desk lamp will direct illumination where it is most needed.

Sawdust, chippings and shavings rapidly accumulate and every carving session should be concluded by brushing up the debris. Apart from being uncomfortable to stand on, heaped wood can be a very real fire risk. Mention of wood waste brings to mind a mishap I have learned to avoid; small deep cavities must never be cleared of waste by blowing into them, unless you include an eye shield in your first aid kit.

1 Wood and woodcarving

You may think that woodcarving is a slight variation on something you have tried before – woodwork. Of course the words are very similar and the two do have some fundamentals in common – for instance, the carver will need to do a certain amount of sawing and planing. But as you immerse yourself in carving, you will begin to appreciate the differences in approach and technique.

The first dissimilarity between the two is the wood used, or rather, its dimensional diversity. Carvers quickly develop a squirrel complex, storing up a variety of pieces regardless of their size and species. This attitude to wood stems from the well founded premise that every piece of wood has modelling potential. Indeed, the pleasurable uncertainty of not knowing what to carve is nearly always resolved by whatever stock there is on hand. Apart from ensuring that you are never stuck for material, making the subject fit the wood is valuable training, and helps develop that flexibility of approach which is essential to original design.

Which wood?

The woodcarver can indulge himself by working with a wide range of timber. To a certain extent, every tree has possibilities for the carver, though naturally some species are more pleasant to work with than others. However, an easily carvable wood, such as lime, will not suit every type of subject and sometimes one virtue cancels out another. An ideal working wood may lack the necessary quality of grain figuration. In carving a delicate shape, the wood's strength may be the first consideration.

The classification of trees into hard and softwoods can be confusing; balsa, for example, is recognised as a 'hardwood'. For practical purposes, I will use the word hard in relation to the level of resistance a cutting tool would meet on a particular kind of wood. Oak, for example, despite its historic connections with carving, is a wood the beginner should avoid because of its inherent toughness and unpredictable grain texture. But you should never dismiss any one timber without pausing to explore its possibilities; see p. iv for more information about the different kinds of timber widely available in Great Britain.

Coarse, stringy, interlocked grain will prove unco-operative with the sharpest chisel and the soundest technique, while a finely textured wood of medium hardness will permit clean chipping from any direction, and allow you to give your complete attention to the shape of the model. If, however, you have little practical experience of wood, you can only experiment with unidentified timber and see what happens.

The most widely available imported timber comes from West Africa: sapele (sap-eel-ee), utile (you-til-ee), makore (mak-or-ree) and obeche (o-beesh-ee or o-beek-ee). The first three, which are mahoganies, are of a red brown colour and the last is pale yellow. All are of medium hardness. Walnut, sycamore, chestnut, lime, oak, plane and yew are not stocked so extensively and are usually only available from specialist timber suppliers. You can order by post.

Obtaining wood

Just how easy (or hard) it is for you to acquire suitable timber will depend on where you live. Without a sawmill in the area or a joinery business to supply off-cuts (short waste ends), you must look to the less direct sources. Old-fashioned solid wooden furniture can usually be purchased for a fraction of its material value, and it is nearly always made from a species that is suitable for carving. Energetic effort will be necessary to remove well established polish and long standing grime. Wood of this kind does have the virtue of being completely inert; it will not be likely to shrink, curl or split, which is a problem you may come across with younger wood.

The coastline is a rewarding hunting ground for hardwood. Timber boats carry a high load of deck cargo and, inevitably, odd planks abandon ship and find their own way home. A rinse down with fresh water is usually sufficient to remove salt deposit.

If you require a particular size of a particular species of wood, you can order it from one of the suppliers advertising in woodworking magazines. Naturally, this method will work out rather more expensive than buying locally because of the postal charge incurred, but the wood is usually of very good quality.

It may seem that the most obvious way of obtaining wood is simply to saw it off a tree. Generally, freshly sawn timber requires long and careful preparation before it can be handled as 'normal' wood. Without experience and knowledge, seasoning any species is a very hit-and-miss business, and if you do intend to try this yourself, get advice before you set about it.

2 Tools

The work-top

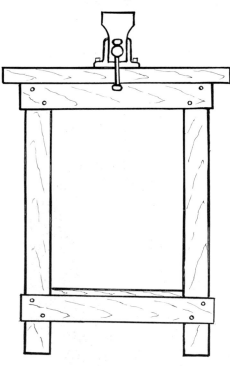

A simple 'knock-up' carver's bench; the position of the vice is a matter of personal choice.

Without a good solid work-top, any attempt to carve would be a shaky proposition. In the old days, a discarded table or chest of drawers could be utilised to act as a bench, but contemporary furniture is not so adaptable. A purpose-built carving bench has little in common with the type used for general woodworking; its main object is to support a vice at a height convenient to the carver and his work. This is usually about 81 cm (2 ft 8 in.) from floor level; if the carver is prepared to make his own bench it can be constructed to suit his own height requirements. Softwood is more likely to be available than hardwood, but this will not matter providing the dimensions of the work bench are not skimped. Four stout legs are the principle components, made from timber not less than 9 cm by 9 cm ($3\frac{1}{2}$ in. by $3\frac{1}{2}$ in.). A square shaped frame will provide all round stability. Jointed rails will require skilled know-how to construct, but the robust dimensions of the wood will permit the use of strong wood screws throughout.

The working surface is best made from 5 cm (2 in.) plank; in this case the use of softwood is advantageous, as it has a frictional quality which is useful when holding down relief work. The work-top should be flush on the front edge, and the three remaining edges should overhang the frame by 6.3 cm ($2\frac{1}{2}$ in.) to facilitate the use of G cramps when holding a wide, flat panel of wood. A shelf supported by the lower rails will further assist the weight/strength factor. The area of the bench-top will be determined by whatever space is available for you to work in.

The vice

Because a normal woodworking vice is wholly unsuitable for woodcarving, the carver must employ the type used by engineers. Generally, a model with 9 cm ($3\frac{1}{2}$ in.) jaws and opening up to 14 cm ($5\frac{1}{2}$ in.) is more than adequate for carvings of average size. Larger versions may possess a rapid adjustment lever or swivel head. Irrespective of these refinements, every engineers' vice is fitted with jaw plates which are rebated into the jaws proper, and secured with countersunk screws. As the object of the vice is to grip the work-piece, these plates are grooved with a diamond pattern for non-slip effect. When work in a more finished state is to be gripped, it will prove necessary to protect it from plate marking. Thin metal angles, a fold of glass paper or nylon jaw covers will all prevent unwanted plate impressions.

Apart from the vice, there are other less static tools for holding work while it is being carved. The quick manoeuvrability of the G cramp makes it ideal for work that must be constantly repositioned. Employed properly, a couple of these cramps are a secure means of holding down a job. A pair that will take in a thickness of 13 cm (5 in.) should accommodate a fair assortment of work. Another handy variation of cramp is the bench holdfast. Whereas the G cramp can only be effective under and over the bench edge, the holdfast can be situated anywhere on the bench top and is especially useful when working with wide panels.

An engineer's vice and G cramps, two methods of holding a workpiece.

General purpose tools

Unless you are in the happy position of being able to purchase wood cut to the required size, a smoothing plane is always the first tool to be used. Some slight adjustment to the wood thickness is usually necessary before starting a relief carving, and this tool is also useful for cleaning second-hand wood.

A few sizes of conventional flat woodworking chisels, preferably of the bevel edge type are also invaluable for edge trimming the waste from an outline.

The removal of outline waste from a design of complex shape is a problem that confounds every beginner. When the timber is as much as 7.5 cm (3 in.) thick this initial hurdle may appear insurmountable. A quick solution is to use a band-saw, but unfortunately this piece of equipment is expensive and needs housing in a permanent workshop. In fact, the profiling of a model plays little part in the actual carving and does not justify substantial outlay. A combination saw set will handle the straightforward sawing jobs that crop up, and a coping saw is capable of circum-navigating shapes of up to 20 mm ($\frac{3}{4}$ in.) thickness. Wood of deeper dimensions must be approached in a less direct manner, which is explained in chapter 3.

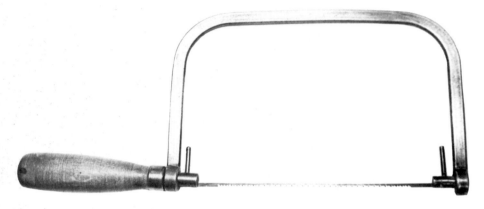

A coping saw.

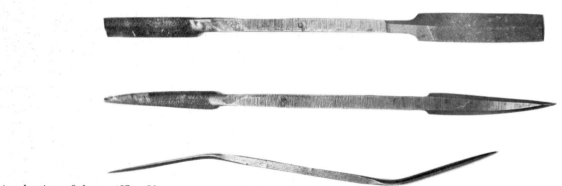

A selection of three riffler files.

Files are now an accepted part of the carver's tool kit, though there was a time when rubbing a carving into shape was frowned upon. Two files that will cope with most situations are a round and half round of 20 cm (8 in.) 'bastard' cut. These shapes will clean off small to large curves and round over a straight edge. Among the more specialised files are the riffler variety, which are especially useful for shaping surface contours. The range of shaper files has opened up an entirely new concept of filing. Here the gradual abrasive quality of the conventional file is replaced by a blade with open cutting teeth and a cutting action that removes waste more rapidly. For work of vigorous design this type of file is extremely satisfying to use.

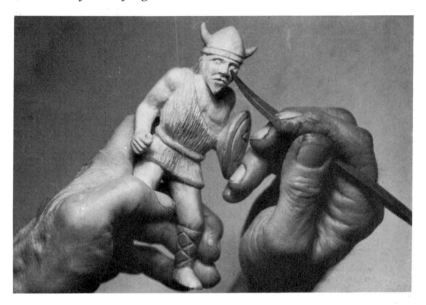

Modelling detail on a small model with a riffler file.

The teeth of a conventional file (left) and (right) open teeth of the shaper file.

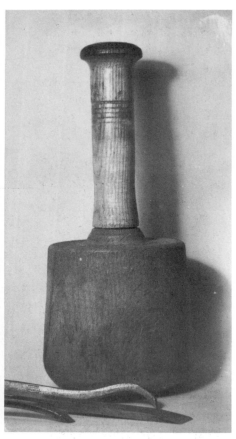

A carver's mallet.

A round mallet is used for carving, and this tool is obtainable in different species of wood and various weights. The weight is not quite so important as the feeling of being at one with a mallet that suits your wrist strength. After thirty minutes of gentle swinging the lightest of mallets insidiously doubles its weight.

The next item of equipment will appeal to readers who like to save time and effort. An electric drill may not seem to have much affinity with woodcarving, but nevertheless its muscle power can be called upon to do many variations on the initial spadework. Used only on wood, a modest set of carbon drills or the more expensive high speed drills will last a lifetime. To start with a range of bit sizes from 2 mm ($\frac{1}{16}$ in.) to 6 mm ($\frac{1}{4}$ in.) should be adequate.

With the practical experience of a few models behind you, you will very soon acquire many additions to your tool kit. Frosting (or matting) punches, for example, will almost certainly be useful in some types of work. Designed to indent a plain surface for contrast texture, they provide interest to background, clothing and decorative relief carving. The punch impressions vary from a single dot to collective groups of very fine spikes. There are other less frequently used punch patterns.

Another important finishing tool is the scraper, and the type I use can be thrown away after use. A local glazier keeps me supplied with waste margins of glass which make very efficient scrapers when snapped across into small lengths.

Dotting the grass with a ball-headed punch (mahogany relief carving).

About chisels

Carving chisels are manufactured to handle every technical requirement of the craft. But as with every other purpose-made tool, if you do not know how to use each chisel to its best advantage, the result will inevitably be disappointing.

There are hundreds of carving chisels to choose from. No doubt the proliferation can be attributed to the needs of bygone carvers and the complexity of their work. This is interesting, but it makes the initial choice of chisels difficult for anyone unfamiliar with the craft.

Among the profusion of chisels the beginner can draw comfort from the fact that they have all evolved from just three variations of 'cut'. This concerns the tip section of the blade. If each of the three principal shapes of chisel are stabbed vertically into a piece of wood, their tip impressions will be straight, curved and V-shaped. Now, if you alter each section to a greater or lesser extent, vary the shape of the blade length, and multiply both these factors by the overall sizes of chisels, you will appreciate why there are so many chisels to choose from.

Most manufacturers market a fair working selection of their

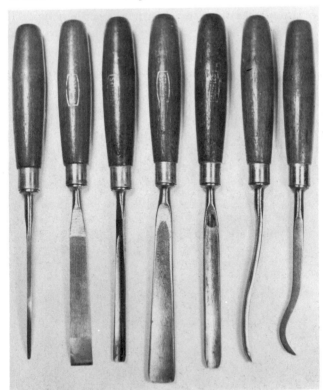

A medium set of carving chisels.

Small carving chisels, for hand pressure only.

chisels neatly boxed (though not ready for immediate use – new chisels of any description are never retailed honed). Any additions can be made from the comprehensive lists supplied by manufacturers, wherein each chisel is listed by name and blade width, and is also identifiable by means of a numbering system which indicates its sectional shape and length.

It is possible to purchase carving chisels with or without handles, which is a convenience as even with fair wear the handles usually outlast their tool iron. Fitting a handle requires the drilling of a straight pilot hole, dead centre into the handle. The hole should be of slightly larger diameter than the tapered tip of the tang, and of a depth commensurate with the length of the tang. Now the hole must be counterbored with progressively larger drills to enable the taper to be fitted in tightly. Ideally, it should be possible to push the handle halfway home before gripping the tool in a vice and firmly tapping the handle down to the shoulder of the tang. (A loose fitting chisel handle is extremely dangerous. If the preliminary drilling out has proved to be excessive, the bore can be blocked in with resin filler paste before inserting the tang. Always allow a generous hardening off period.)

Every carver has at least one favourite gouge for prolonged mallet work. This should be fitted with a boxwood handle separated from the tool shoulder with a shock-absorbent leather washer. Ash handles are perfectly adequate for tools subject only to hand pressure or very light mallet force.

Knowing why you need any particular tool is the best way of building up a tool kit and obtaining full value from it. Undoubtedly, the workhorse of carving chisels is the gouge, which will rough off waste in any direction without splitting the wood. It can, of course, be employed on fine modelling. One or two sizes and shapes of this tool will handle an infinite range of subject matter (providing the work load is not beyond their working capacity).

The sectional curvature or sweep of carving gouges caters for a deep or shallow cut. To some extent a 'middle of the road' gouge (regular sweep) can be manipulated to cut a variety of depths and widths. However, if you want to diminish the width of a groove,

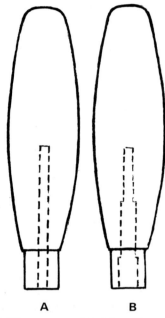

A   **B**

Drilling a new chisel handle.
A: pilot bore; B: counter bore(s).

Carving gouges – the long and the short.

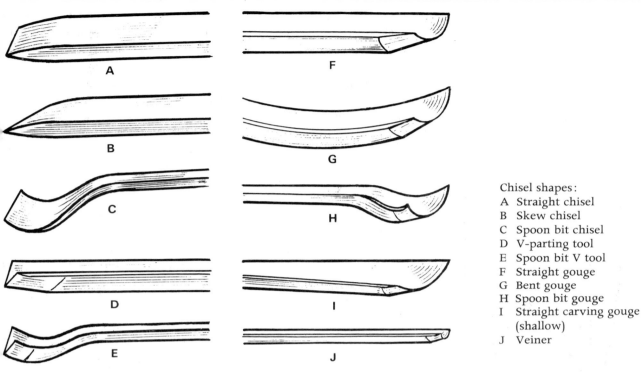

Chisel shapes:
A Straight chisel
B Skew chisel
C Spoon bit chisel
D V-parting tool
E Spoon bit V tool
F Straight gouge
G Bent gouge
H Spoon bit gouge
I Straight carving gouge (shallow)
J Veiner

Sectional shapes of gouges and V parting tools.

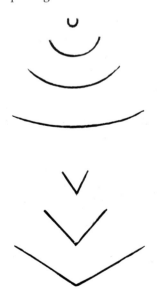

but make it deeper, you can only achieve this with a smaller version of the tool. Grooves of a distinct U-shape, large or small, are made by fluters and veiners. Unlike other types of gouge cut, this kind of grooving is primarily intended for decorative purposes.

Like the gouge family, V-parting tools are straight, bent or spoon-ended. Similarly again, their sectional V-shape is available in a range of sizes, each with three variations of cutting angle: acute, medium or obtuse. V-parting tools are used to cut a groove of uniform width and depth by simply moving the chisel forwards – as opposed to developing a groove with a conventional flat chisel by notching out the veeing from an overhead standpoint, or manipulating a chisel corner to part the wood from either side of a given line.

How successfully this tool works will depend largely on the nature of the wood. Close-packed hardwood such as sycamore and beech permit greater manoeuvrability when the cutting action is directed across the grain. Used similarly on softwood, the grain will show a tearing effect.

The carver's straight or flat chisel has a double-sided cutting bevel. This feature also applies to the skew chisel, which is angled off across its width to make a sharp point on one corner. The method of tapering the blade to a cutting edge is designed to neutralise the 'bite'. In contrast to the cutting action of a conventional chisel, the carver's chisel will be inclined to chip the wood rather than to pare it. It also has certain advantages when working on inside curves or when 'setting in' (stabbing) a line drawing for a relief carving (see page 31). Here the double-sided cutting bevel will show less tendency than the single-sided version to drift away from the line, a problem which may sometimes occur due to grain formation.

Numerous tools which are used less frequently will be acquired as your work gradually progresses. Every carving chisel requires a degree of technical skill, some considerably more than others. Possessing the correct tool for the job does not necessarily mean that it will be applied to its best advantage. It is always with the greatest reluctance that I swap a warm chisel for a cold one. More important than variety is the working efficiency of whatever tools you have to start with. Just one correctly honed chisel is worth half a dozen tools of mediocre performance.

Honing the chisel

The cutting edge of a wood chisel is made up from two angles or bevels on the end of the blade width. A new chisel will only have the broader of these angles, the ground bevel, applied to its tip. (It is called the ground bevel because the metal has been removed by a grindstone.) Before the chisel will cut, a secondary angle, the cutting edge, must be honed on the extreme tip.

The process of honing is carried out on a flat sharpening stone (an oilstone) made from a finer grade of abrasive grit than that of a grindstone. To reduce its frictional quality, the stone surface must be lightly coated with a thin lubricating oil before honing commences. Although the honing angle is not particularly critical, care should be taken not to position the chisel at too steep an angle. Generally, a holding position that is naturally comfortable produces the most consistent results.

Straight edged chisels are honed by moving the blade backwards and forwards, maintaining a constant angle while applying light firm pressure on the chisel tip. The beginner may at first experience difficulty in applying an even honing pressure, which will result in the chisel having a wedge-shaped cutting tip and consequently an unbalanced cutting action. Frequent inspection of this area should reveal an even honing polish contrasting sharply with the dull ground bevel. A slight 'hooking' of the cutting edge will signify that the steel has been honed to an ultimate degree of fineness. The honing burr (sometimes referred to as the wire) must be removed by gentle blandishing. This involves lightly rubbing the cutting side of the chisel against the stone to straighten the burr, which can then be disposed of completely by running the

Honing a straight chisel.

Blandishing the face of the chisel after honing.

edge over a corner of softwood (chisels with a double ground bevel will require stropping on leather).

Gouges demand similar treatment, but with more animated

Honing a gouge by a slide and turning movement.

movement, depending on their curvature and the nature of the ground bevel. The outside ground gouge, which is the gouge most frequently used, offers a choice of two methods. The first requires the stone to be positioned at a right angle to the honing stance and the tip sharpened by a co-ordinated sliding and rocking movement. This technique is especially suitable for gouges of shallow curvature. The second method involves describing a figure of eight honing pattern, the gouge tip being rocked to accommodate the degree of turn throughout this movement.

Unlike a straight chisel, a gouge requires the attention of an oilstone slip to remove the honing burr. This is a small sharpening stone shaped to fit the inside curvature (or V-section) of the tool. The burr is removed by gently stroking the slip away from the cutting edge. Inside ground gouges must be honed entirely by using a slip; here, slips of varying coarseness are particularly useful.

For honing purposes, V-parting tools can be regarded as straight chisels, each side of the V section receiving the same amount of honing time. A triangular slip is used to finish the edge on the inside of the tool. Irrespective of the blade length and shape, the majority of carving chisels can, with some adjustment of the honing position, be successfully sharpened in the manner described on

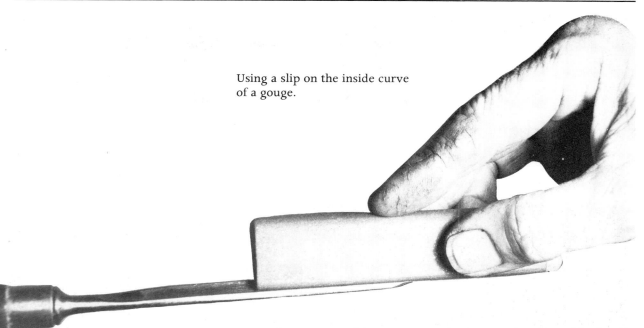

Using a slip on the inside curve
of a gouge.

p. 14 above. Spoon bit gouges require extra attention with the slip
because of the limited space available for honing.

With experience you will begin to appreciate that there are
different degrees of sharpness. A razor blade is the ultimate in a
finely-honed edge, but it is far too fragile to withstand the resistance of hardwood. A chisel edge must be regarded in similar terms.
If softwood such as pine is being carved, the tools can be brought
to a fine degree of sharpness by stropping the edge over a piece of
board-backed leather which has been impregnated with vaseline
and dressed with pumice, fine emery or crocus powder. The edge
must be stroked over the strop against the cutting direction to
prevent it digging into the leather. Gouges can be similarly treated
by placing the leather over a curved piece of wood. It must be
appreciated that stropping will not be effective unless the edge
has been previously honed very keenly on an oilstone.

Grinding the bevel

Every time a chisel is honed the blade length is imperceptibly
shortened and it will eventually be necessary to regrind the cutting
bevel before you can obtain a keen edge. It is more satisfactory
to be equipped for this occasional chore yourself than to have to
ask around for someone to do it for you each time. You can also
adjust the degree of taper on the cutting bevel to suit your taste.

This is one good reason for owning an electric drill; as a source of
power for a small grindstone, it ensures one hundred per cent
efficiency from your tools. The drill can be mounted in a horizontal
position on an accessory stand – or an improvised tool rest (firmly

Progressive wear on a chisel tip when regular grinding has not been carried out.

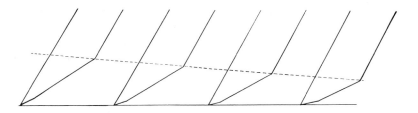

secured) may be used. Before you embark on any sort of high-speed grinding, it is absolutely essential to wear eye protection such as goggles or a face shield.

It is generally possible to get good results by holding the tool lightly but firmly against the side of the stone. The only drawback to dry grinding, as opposed to using a slow turning wet stone, lies in the danger of 'burning' the chisel tip because of the frictional heat generated. When this occurs, a change of colouring (rainbowing) indicates serious interference with the tempering. This problem must *always* be avoided, which can easily be done by frequently cooling the tool in water.

You can also spend time on the grindstone squaring off the ends of any unevenly honed chisel tips. Inside ground gouges can be treated with a small grinding arbor; the tool is held underneath the arbor to enable you to see clearly as you grind.

A small grinding arbor mounted in a drill chuck.

Grinding a gouge with a drill powered grinding stone. Eye protection must be always worn when using a high speed grinder.

18

Holding the tools

The carver confronted with a first-rate piece of wood and unfamiliar tools may well find the experience a perplexing one. Although the obvious place to hold anything is by its handle, woodworking tools respond to any subtle change of grip, pressure or direction. The handle of a tool gives no clue to the extent of its versatility – this is something the craftsman must discover for himself. Indeed, because the human element plays such a large part in tool behaviour, there are no hard to remember instructions on how tools should be held. Unfortunately, however, the simplicity of certain tools permits the beginner to grip the handle confidently with the idea that if it feels comfortable there can be no other way of holding it. This is not the case.

The handle of a deep-bladed saw, for instance, positively begs to be held in a tightly clenched fist. In fact, a straight stabilising index finger will make a world of difference to the progression and accuracy of the saw cut. This minor adjustment also applies when using a coping saw, and the finger tips should be placed lightly on the front of the frame when profiling. (It is possible to re-frame a blade in the coping saw with the cutting action of the teeth in either direction. Correctly, the blade should be positioned to cut when the saw is pushed away from the body.)

Files large and small (rifflers excepted) are two-handed implements. Here the important thing is not so much how to hold the handle, but ensuring that the sharp tang end is equipped with one. Many beginners regard file handles as non-essential, but using these tools without handles is rarely effective and very often dangerous. Handles are inexpensive to buy and easy to fit.

Chisels are very unforgiving when wrongly held, and their variations of shape and cutting abilities cannot be used to advantage

A stabilising index finger will point any deep bladed saw in the right direction.

19

The first and second fingers of the left hand help to restrain and guide the chisel blade.

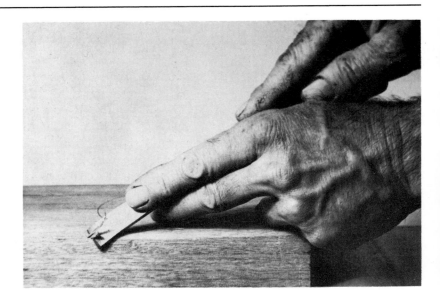

How to hold the chisel when incising wood from a vertical position.

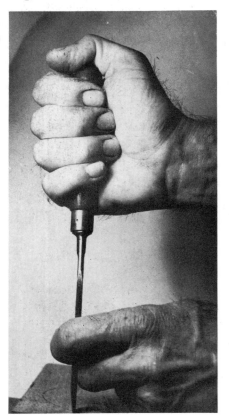

without correct handling. Happily, the right chisel grip is not difficult to acquire and once acquired is never forgotten. Apart from adjustment for the angle of cut, the left hand finger positions are fairly constant when the full blade length is used; the chisel is at all times trapped and guided between the first two fingers of the left hand. The right hand pressure position is less critical; you maintain a comfortable curling finger grip for diagonal working, changing to a full fist with the thumb on top of the handle when the chisel is being used for vertical cutting.

The most natural chisel grip is that which is employed when using a mallet – a full fist around the lower three-quarters of the handle length. Here the feel of the chisel is less important than firm control of it. The mallet is intended for short reflex action knocking; good mallet technique involves sensing the precise degree of force necessary for any given situation. If you gauge the amount of force right and angle the chisel correctly, using the mallet should always result in the removal of a clean decisive chip. Just how often the mallet is used will depend largely on the size and nature of the work. Bowl carving for instance, would be quite impossible without the energetic use of a mallet. On the other hand, small figure or animal studies can only be handled by careful paring off.

A medium-sized set of carving chisels will handle work both above and below the middle-sized range, though obviously tools in keeping with the size of the model will be more comfortable to work with. Large chisels have a surfeit of finger room, and, at the other extreme, small spade tools barely allow orthodox application. However, the delicacy of their purpose must be matched with

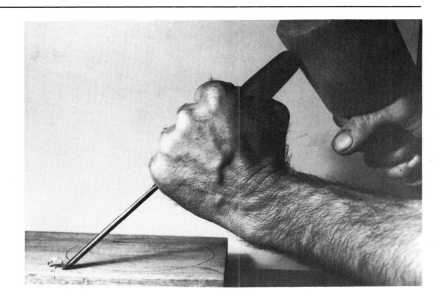

Gripping the chisel for 'square on' connection with the mallet.

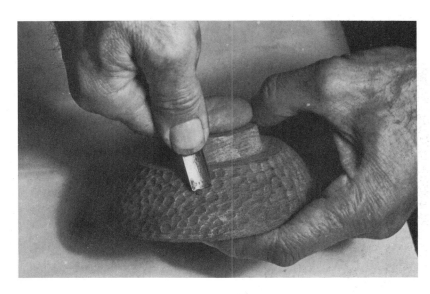

The 'short blade' technique, used here for lightly chipping a base block.

finesse – a combination of restrained pressure and finger tip control should be sufficient for small fine work.

Small spade tools are also handy for lightly chipping a job which requires constant changes of position. Here the tool must be held one-handed with less than half the blade length protruding, and providing the fingers holding the small workpiece are safely out of harm's way, it can be considered safe to make small quickly terminated chippings. Fine paring off can also be done in this manner. Under no circumstances should incisions of a vertical or forceful nature be attempted with the one-handed chisel technique.

3 Outlining and profiling

Planning a model

'I'd like to carve, but I can't draw!' Surprisingly, drawing talent is not an essential foundation for a build-up of three-dimensional modelling skill, as the practical difficulties of transferring neat draughtsmanship from paper onto a portion of bark-covered tree are insurmountable. With raw material such as this, a couple of strategic chalk marks are sufficient to start the job off. When you look at a chunk of unsawn timber you can imagine what a slight effect any drawing ability would have on it. Moreover, the artist rarely maintains any real advantage when the wood has been machined to a more presentable condition.

The carver's immediate concerns are the lines of an illustration that can be sawn or chiselled, and the futility of elaborate marking out becomes apparent when you find that ninety-nine per cent of the surface drawing must be lowered off to relieve one small high point. Whereas the artist draws or paints by a process of addition, a carver can only obtain shape by subtraction. Indeed, now is the time to start remembering that a chipping once removed cannot be put back!

Generally an outline of the subject, usually a side-on view or a profile, is sufficient to start the work in the right direction. It is a very uncommon subject that cannot be found and copied from some existing photograph or line drawing. A word of caution, though – a dramatic picture does not necessarily make a spectacular woodcarving. Research a few pictures of your subject; one may possess a clear outline but indistinct detail and conversely an otherwise unsuitable picture may show a wealth of detail. A rough sketch incorporating the best features from a selection of photos and drawings will provide valuable acquaintance with the subject matter.

There is always the occasional model that demands extra special care during the planning stage. It may be that the wood to be used is rare and cannot easily be replaced, or it could be that your concept of the subject is less than definite. When you need to take extra care, make a model from plasticine before committing your thoughts to wood. Size is unimportant, and it need not be finished off. Apart from revealing any weakness in structure or design it will point the way for tackling the real thing.

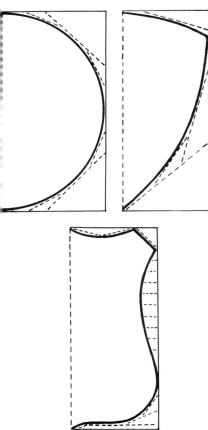

The sketch model in plasticine provides a useful basis for this carving of a tiger mask.

Outside profiling

The dotted lines indicate where the saw cuts will be (using a panel or tenon saw).

From a carver's point of view, the length and breadth of a piece of wood is never quite as important as its thickness. When this dimension is beyond the capacity of hand tools the beginner usually comes to terms with the problem by confining his ambitions to timber of less daunting proportions. If the chosen subject has a complex outline, the thickness problem is aggravated further. On the other hand, a simple outline of reasonable depth may prove difficult to profile because of the hard texture of the wood. There is no one hard and fast formula for the removal of waste wood, for every shape will require its own particular profiling technique. It may be some consolation to mention that a machine tool which can handle every aspect of this spadework has yet to be invented.

Timber thickness permitting, a coping saw will, unassisted, accomplish a fair proportion of profiling jobs. Light and easy to use, with quick inexpensive blade replacements, this little saw will cut an amazing variety of materials.

The waste wood surrounding an outline may usually be sawn away until it can be trimmed off with a conventional (flat) chisel. Here the workpiece is laid flat on its side, and the chisel strokes are made in a vertical direction across the edge grain. If you wish to get a more finished outline, hold the work in a vice and file the edges. The shaper file is particularly useful in this respect; the round version of the tool is able to cope with deep channels and any irregularly shaped apertures which may require adjustment. For smaller work, conventional files offer a smoother and more gradual reduction of waste wood.

Using a normal saw and a chisel is just one method of profiling. Another approach which is especially suitable for dealing with thick wood is to perforate the outline with a series of holes. Here, using an electric drill dispenses with the physical labour and it

23

will not be the least fatigued by the hardest of hardwood. Chain (or link) drilling will not dispose of waste wood entirely on its own, however. The perforations must be pierced at their weakest point with a coping saw before the surrounding waste is finally released. This process will leave the edge of the model with pointed corrugations which can be cleaned off fairly quickly with a chisel.

The ideal drill size for wood no thicker than 51 mm (2 in.) is 5 mm ($\frac{3}{16}$ in.). Although a drill of larger dimensions will cover

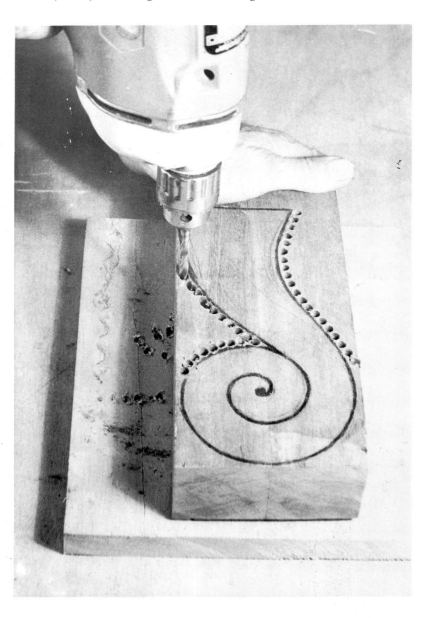

An electric drill used for profiling a thick shape.

Trimming off the drill serrations.

The drill fitted with a dowel
sleeve.

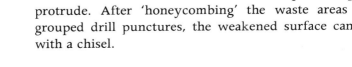

ground more rapidly and, if need be, bore a greater depth of wood,
the corrugations that remain after sawing will require more time
and effort to remove. A drill of diameter less than $\frac{3}{16}$ in. will not
bore deeply enough nor will it clear itself of the impacted bore
waste so readily.

Any variation of drill size is permissible when the outline is in
relief, for here the waste can neither be sawn nor completely
drilled through. It can, however, be weakened by 'stop' drilling
the surface with a drill bit fitted with an adaptation to govern the
depth of its penetration. This need be nothing more complicated
than a dowel sleeve which allows the required depth of drill to
protrude. After 'honeycombing' the waste areas with closely
grouped drill punctures, the weakened surface can be lifted off
with a chisel.

25

Inside profiling

The need for internal profiling frequently occurs when the limbs of a subject enclose waste that cannot be removed by sawing from the outside edge. A coping saw is ideal for this sort of work. By disengaging the blade from the saw frame it can be threaded through a hole drilled in the waste, re-tensioned and manipulated to cut the required aperture.

A much larger version of the frame saw, the bow saw, is specifically designed for woodcutting. Its robust cutting action can prove invaluable on work of large external curvature; however, since it is equipped with a much heavier blade than the coping saw its twine tensioned hardwood frame can be rather unwieldy to handle on an outline that demands frequent changes of direction. Disengaging the blade for internal profiling can also be a time-consuming business.

Inside apertures are cleaned out in a similar manner to that used for the external edge, though really small openings are best left until the wood thickness has been reduced. Acute inside angles should be cleaned with a sharp-edged file.

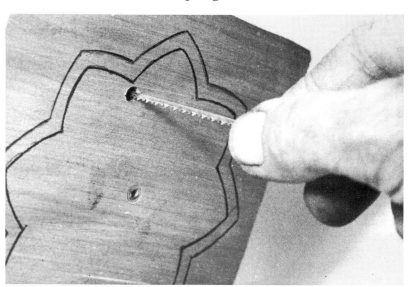

A coping saw blade threaded through the waste area which is to be profiled.

Often the beginner will set his tools an impossible task by drawing an outline he has been hard put to achieve with a pencil. Delicate protrusions and tiny inside apertures should be avoided or left until the vigorous spadework has been completed. Nothing is quite so disheartening as having to glue a model together before carving has even started when one did not intend to have to do so; (sometimes, of course it is necessary to glue pieces together to make up a required width or depth of wood before profiling).

4 Securing a carving

Securing a carving

Although it is necessary that wood is held firmly for sawing and drilling, this does not mean that the same methods of retention should be used when carving. The saw and drill are both held at a constant working angle, and their behaviour rarely produces any surprises, but the movement of carving chisels will be more diverse, subject to changes of direction, grain texture and working pressure. A device that maintains an adequate grip when the work is being tackled from one direction may suddenly prove inadequate when subject to pressure from a different angle.

No matter how secure the fastening may seem, an experienced carver will never assume that the workpiece is immovable. Every carver should take the simple precaution of keeping hands and fingers behind the chisel tip, so as to avoid any injury. However, very small models may need to be held by hand as described on p. 21. In such cases there is often very slight physical exertion and a chisel technique is used which reduces the risk of injury to less than that met when using a small penknife.

Securing a board

The two principal groups of carving work, 'relief' and 'round', start life as a board or a block respectively. A board is less of a security risk because of its flat surface area. G cramps are a quick reliable means of holding a board secure against the bench top, though never less than two should be used. Unfortunately, even when reversed to accommodate their screw length underneath the bench edge, G cramps may prove obstructive to low angle chisel work – or the model may be too delicate to withstand effective holding pressure on its edge. This irritation can easily be disposed of by mounting the workpiece on an inert base board of greater width (plywood or block board will do). After screws have been entered through the base board into what will be the high areas of the relief carving, the board's perimeter will allow for free and easy positioning of G cramps.

There will be the odd occasion when it will prove necessary to dispense with G cramps completely. When the work has to be secured without mechanical assistance, a convenient method is to frame the workpiece inside three battens which are screwed down on the bench top, the fourth side of the frame being positioned to

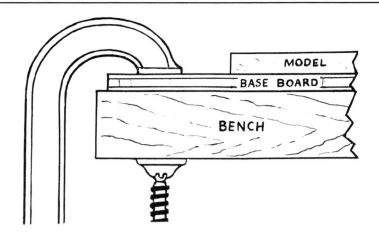

Cramping the base board of the workpiece.

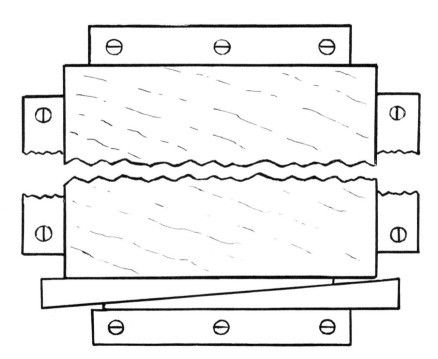

How to set up the workpiece for frame wedging.

permit the entry of two long tapered opposing wedges. When knocked against each other, these will have the effect of squeezing the workpiece tightly inside the frame. This method is only suitable for straight-sided shapes.

Metal clips, however, are the complete answer for any shape of relief work and you will find it well worth your while to build up a selection of clip sizes. A set of six is usually sufficient to hold down work of average size, though this number can be adjusted to accommodate the actual board area. When in doubt, use two too many. If you want to make the clips yourself, you must start with a strip of 25 mm (1 in.) by 3 mm ($\frac{1}{8}$ in.) malleable iron. To ascertain the exact length to be bent, a mock-up clip made from soft tin should be tried against the work thickness. After straightening the mock-up clip, its length can be marked off on the heavier metal and the pieces cut accordingly. Once bent to shape, each clip can then be drilled to accept a no. 10 round head wood screw.

Work that lacks the strength and substance to withstand entry of screws or pressure clips, such as a length of reproduction moulding, will have to be indirectly glued to the base board. This can be done by gluing paper on the underside of the workpiece which is then smeared with glue before being left to set on the base board. When the carving is completed a thin sharp blade inserted between the glued joint will prize the work off the board. Any paper adhering to the workpiece can be soaked off with a wet rag. Only glue that is soluble with water should be used.

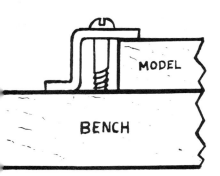

Workpiece clipped to the benchtop.

Securing a block

If you are working on a model 'in the round', the wood must be secured in an upright or horizontal working position. In either case, the leverage on the fixing will be considerably greater than that of a relief carving. The most obvious means of holding a block is the vice, and, with certain reservations, this will afford the best variety of working positions. A swivel-headed type of vice is even more versatile and is capable of swinging the work from one

The advantage of a natural base is clear from this little model. In spite of having only a toe hold, the figure can be worked on comfortably.

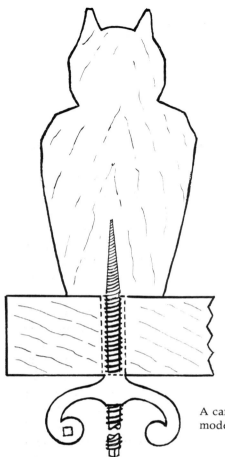

side to the other, though being able to position the work conveniently will not necessarily mean that the grain direction will be changed to the carver's advantage.

The side grip of vice jaws can only be effective when the workpiece is solid enough to withstand the pressure. During the early stages of development this problem may not be apparent, but as the model progresses it may assume a shape that cannot comfortably be held in the vice jaws, or which lacks the necessary strength to be gripped in this way. This difficulty can be eliminated by constructing the model with a natural base; the solid wood will provide a reliable holding point throughout the whole course of the work.

It is not always possible, or desirable, to integrate a base with the original design. Without side pressure to secure the work the only other alternative is to attach the job to the work-top. The easiest way of doing that is to use a carver's screw, which is a length of strongly threaded bar with a free running wing nut. One end is tapered off to make a gimlet point for entering into the workpiece, while the other end is squared to match a spanner hole in the wing nut for tightening the screw in the model. The screw can be used by passing it either through a hole in the benchtop, or through a separate block of waste wood which can be held in the vice.

A carver's screw inserted in a model.

5 Relief carving

Whereas 'in the round' carving requires wood of fairly substantial girth, relief work can be adjusted to suit any thickness of timber, which makes it slightly more popular than other types of carving. There is less need for energetic profiling and constant adjustment of the work. It is not necessary to view the model from the back or to line up features on opposite sides. But these minor practical benefits do not mean that relief carving is a less skilful art form, quite the contrary. More finely carved content can be packed into a small slim panel than may be worked from a block of monolithic proportions.

Anyone who enjoys careful planning will find relief work offers opportunity for methodical thinking. The more adventurous may prefer a less disciplined approach: you start with a quick sketch, finish with a high polish and an idea is realised in the beauty of wood. Whatever the approach, the operative word is 'sketch', for any temptation to use the wood as a scribbling block should be resisted. Preliminary drawings are always more successfully developed on paper of a size and shape which matches the area of the wood surface. If the job is symmetrical, such as a shield, half the outline can be drawn and the paper folded down a centre line to duplicate the other half accurately. Work of this nature should be profiled to shape before you embark on the surface design.

Tracing and raising the outline

When the initial drawing is considered satisfactory it can be reproduced on the wood by means of carbon paper. To avoid the frustration of inadvertently moving the copy out of line with the carbon, the paper is best pinned down on the wood. A complex tracing must be tackled in a methodical manner; jumping from one part of the drawing to another will only result in an incomplete tracing when the paper is removed. Before any of the waste areas of wood can be lowered off, it will be necessary to incise the design by penetrative stabbing with a chisel. Ideally, the angle of cut should lean a few degrees off the vertical towards the waste side of the line.

Unless the wood is particularly hard, this process must never be started with a mallet; apart from possible inaccuracy of cut, there is always a real danger of splitting the wood. In any event, this tool

31

Profiling the outline.

Rounding off the edge.

Tracing off a securely pinned
drawing.

The workpiece is now ready for
carving.

should only ever be employed with the minimum of force. Quite sufficient pressure can be obtained with a firm two-handed grip on the chisel. You will find that as you change direction, you meet different levels of resistance to chisel penetration. Resistance will be greater and penetration less when working across the grain; when working down grain, penetration is easier. It takes practice to maintain an even depth of cut. A little extra push will be called for when using the sectional shape of a wide gouge to circum-navigate a curve. Long straight incisions such as a border margin, are best inscribed with a sharp point to provide a firm guide for locating the chisel tip before any pressure is applied.

Sinking the background

Lowering off or 'sinking' the background can start when the border and outer periphery of the subject matter has been isolated to some degree from the waste areas. The type of tool used for removing the waste will depend on the space available. Very

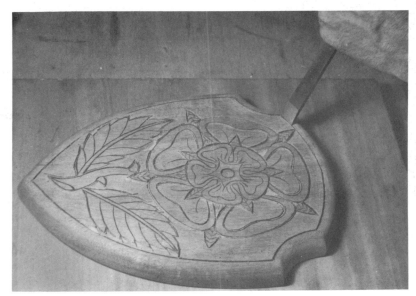

Incising the surface drawing using a straight chisel.

The corners are stabbed with a matching section of gouge.

narrow passages of waste will spring out of their own volition or require very little persuasion to be lifted out with a narrow chisel reversed to work on its ground bevel. These loose chips will convey some idea of how deep the vertical incisions have penetrated and help you find the angle required for the chisel when tackling the broader areas of waste. A flat conventional chisel can be used to slope off a small margin of waste down to the edge of the vertical incision. This will permit a shallow gouge to rough out the raised area without running into the subject matter or frame wall.

If the intention is only lightly to relieve the subject to a two-dimensional state, then the depth acquired from one 'setting back' may be sufficient. This will not permit any vigorous modelling of

The background is lowered.

the surface area other than perhaps the inclusion of incised lines. If you wish to sink the background to the maximum depth, you will have to repeat the process until the relief effect is heavy enough to be itself relieved. At this stage the ground work can be brought to a near finished condition by gently planing off what the gouge has roughed out either with a flat chisel worked on its ground bevel or with a straight carving chisel. The outline of the subject will also benefit from more precise trimming of its now exposed edge. Similarly, the inside of the frame wall will almost certainly require attention from a chisel.

A successful relief carving should deceive the eye into believing that its three-dimensional quality is far greater than it really is. Unfortunately, the first victim of this illusion is usually the carver himself. Irrespective of how high the relieved blank appears to be standing, its thickness will diminish with alarming rapidity after the foremost high points have been relieved. 'Running out of wood' is a common and disheartening experience for many beginners and is always due to over-attention to one particular detail. It could happen with the profile of a face; the ear, being the highest point, is obviously the first feature that must be relieved. But instead of lightly raising this protuberance, nearly half the available thickness is expended. Not surprisingly, the finished profile is somewhat unusual because the eye, nose and lips are on one level, and the ear predominates in extra heavy relief.

This inadvertent surrealism can be avoided; you should try and visualise the finished carving cut across its centre to expose the sectional shape. Then, make a rough sketch showing the steps, bulges and undulations that must be contained in the thickness of wood available for relief. Although this sketch cannot be regarded as a working drawing, it will help you see the limitations of the material.

Making the vertical incisions of the surface illustration must be a more precise, gentle procedure than the brisk stabbing of the outline. Under no circumstances should any attempt be made to round off part of the model until every feature of the job has been relieved – premature modelling is a sure way of losing sight of basic proportions. Concave cavities must be tackled straight off the line without any preliminary incising to isolate the waste. A straight gouge will start the cavity, and then a bent or spoon bit tool is used depending on the depth required.

As with all carved work, best results are obtained by keeping the model in a fluid state; a methodical untidiness should prevail until the shape has resolved itself. After a final check and trim of the relieved layers where necessary, a straight flat chisel may be used

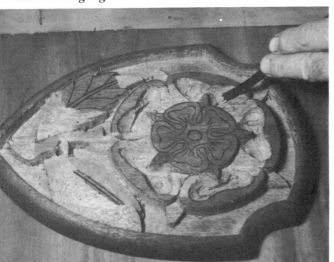

Roughing out the larger cavities with a bent gouge.

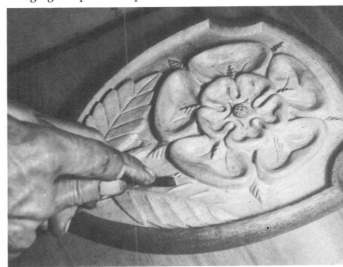

Gouging out precise depressions.

to take the edge off all the sharp corners. Like the previous stages of work this rounding off must be evenly distributed over the model to provide a clear picture of shape development. The cutting action should be of a light paring nature, made with appreciation of the grain direction.

To facilitate the rounding off, re-position the baseboard so as to gain a comfortable working position. The chisel cannot round off a corner to a state of perfection, and any tiny *'flats'* remaining can be blended into the overall roundness with a small file.

Finishing the carving

The time and effort spent on finishing a model is generally directed towards obtaining a smooth unblemished surface. Apart from being an accepted standard of contemporary craftsmanship, a well finished surface will show the grain figuration to its best advantage, and will provide a good foundation for most types of surface coating.

Certain types of subject matter will benefit from unrestrained glass-papering. A smooth flowing impressionistic study of a bird or fish would fit this category. On the other hand, a decorative panel of sharply defined detail would not be enhanced by blurring over the high points and corners with glass-paper. Understandably, the beginner is always eager to smooth out the wrinkles in a model, whereas the experienced carver will regard glass-paper as a tool, to be used with skill and discretion.

Glass-paper is manufactured in a variety of abrasive gradations; the grade of M2 is coarse enough to start with. As the surface is evened off you can progress to the more flexible sheets of fine and very fine grades.

A scraper will remove a very fine shaving of wood when pulled across the grain of a surface which is already in a semi-smooth condition. Its action is dependent on the sharp corner across its blade width. Large scrapers for conventional woodwork can be sharpened for this use, but usually small improvised versions of the tool are sufficient for carving purposes. Glass strip is very effective for flat surfaces, while pieces of hacksaw blade can be ground to accommodate curves.

When nothing less than a perfectly flat surface will suffice and the area in question is fenced in with a raised border, a surface gauge can be made from a scrap piece of wood. By removing a corner of the wood an overhanging arm is made to accommodate a loose sliding pin, which will rise and fall when moved over any humps or hollows. A piece of white card mounted on one side of the pin with graduations marked on it will help you to see the varying levels of the wood as the pin is moved over the surface. There is also a variation of this method, whereby a sharp pointed

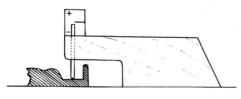

A loose pin surface gauge.

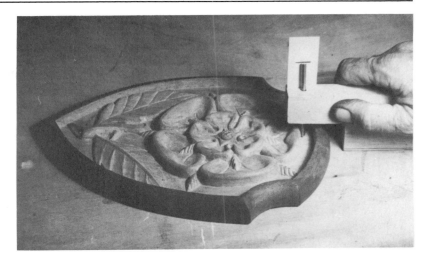

Checking the background level with a loose pin surface gauge.

The finished model (mahogany).

'fixed' pin is used which scratches the high spots. Either type of gauge will only be effective when used on a level base board.

Misericords, carved in oak, from
St Nicholas Chapel, King's Lynn
(about 1415).

A settle end, carved in oak by
George Tack, teacher of
woodcarving at the Royal College
of Art from 1901–1924.

38

Dramatic relief carving of an eagle, by a 15-year-old secondary school student.

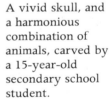

A 'heraldic beast', carved by a 14-year-old secondary school student.

SAINT THOMAS MORE

P
R
A
Y
+
F
O
R
+
U
S

A vivid skull, and a harmonious combination of animals, carved by a 15-year-old secondary school student.

An oak carving by Peter Etheredge from the Church of St Thomas More Cheltenham.

The profile relief

A profiled relief, carved in walnut.

Sloped relief work

Nowadays, surface embellishment is appreciated for its decorative value as well as for the traditional craftsmanship involved. Carving in relief from one piece of board is no longer the rule that it used to be; the introduction of new materials has done much to change the concept of relief carving and today's carver may dispense with the setting-in procedure, starting work with a profile cut-out of the subject. Licence to cut corners is, to some extent, justified by the flawless perfection of modern laminates which, when used as a background, complement a natural wood carving and also provide a contrast of colour, something relief carving has always been short of (unless you resort to staining the background, a practice I cannot recommend).

Handling a profile relief is very similar to the practice described earlier, the outline being screwed to a baseboard and developed to an advanced state of modelling. An easily identifiable outline is preferable to a larger, less defined subject. Edge detail can be finished off freely with files and glass-paper as the outline is not confined within a border. There are certain limitations with this style of work; fragile protrusions should be avoided unless their length is strengthened by grain direction.

The addition of a frame does not offer the free choice of background shape as would a solid board carving. Laminates need gluing to a rigid backing and care must be taken to ensure that the material used for this purpose is entirely inert, and not likely to twist or bow at some future date.

'Sloped' relief is another quick method of raising surface design. This type of light decoration can be carved with a minimum of tools and preparation. The approach is less ambitious than with more complex relief work, and indeed, success depends on the carver resisting any inclination to (literally) go deeper into the subject. This system of carving is an attractive proposition for the craftsman who likes to make the occasional piece of solid wooden furniture, for it involves shallow penetration of the surface without prolonged waste removal. There were times when no piece of furniture was considered worthy of house room unless it was lavishly adorned with swirling scroll work or camouflaged under a profusion of acanthus leaves; used sparingly, however, light sloped relief work strikes a happy medium between the over-decorated and the stark.

Plain uncomplicated outline is absolutely essential to start with. After the outline has been incised, a second outline accurately encompassing and separated from the subject matter by a 10 mm ($\frac{3}{8}$ in.) margin is lightly relieved to a depth of approximately 3 mm

Three styles of flower head in slope relief (parana pine).

($\frac{1}{8}$ in.). This outer chisel work must be of very neat appearance and particular care must be taken not to cut beyond the line of the outer circle. Naturally, the surface modelling of the shapes cannot be heavy, so you should employ a design that will compensate for this lack of depth. Clean decisive line work will both add definition and provide greater dimension, which is helpful when using wood that is not normally acceptable for carving, which may be the case if you are carving on furniture.

Any departure from the original methods of relief carving will bring about certain limitations, so having decided on the choice of subject, you should give serious consideration as to what will prove the most effective method of treatment. If the composition contains detail and the finished result must appear fully modelled, nothing less than a genuine relief job will do. When the subject can be up-dated into a piece of eye-catching decor, profiled relief will allow free interpretation. For the craftsman with divided interests who wants to make a box lid or blank expanse of panel look less monotonous, the sloped relief technique is worth cultivating.

6 Letter carving

There is a certain dignity to words carved in wood, though they may only be the nameplate of a house, boat or hotel. It is a very satisfying job to do, too.

The main object, of course, is to sink or raise the letters in wood. Start by planning out the letters on paper before tracing them onto the wood. While no one is likely to notice slight deviations in letter design or fractionally less than exact spacing, consistency of style must be maintained. A book of alphabets is essential for both the capitals and the lower case letters and numerals. Not every alphabet will lend itself to being transcribed for carving, and the beginner should start with letters of clean open design and square finished stems. Fine intersections and flamboyant flourishes should be avoided; these styles are possible if cut out very shallow, but they are difficult.

The best species of wood for this type of work will depend largely on the work size. Fairly hard close-grained timber is ideal for small to medium sized work, while a really large display would be easier to handle in yellow pine or a similar softwood. Generally, incised lettering can be executed in almost any species of timber, though teak and mahogany are particularly suitable when the job is intended for a lifetime of out of door wear and tear.

Wood for the average nameplate should be in the region of 19 mm ($\frac{3}{4}$ in.) thick. There are no special chisels for letter carving. Contrary to what may be the first impression, the V-parting tool is a far from ideal chisel for incised lettering. Unlike the gouge, which can be used to good effect across the grain, V tools are less easy to control and inclined to leave evidence of tearing on the surface edge. In any event, launching into a letter cutting job without any careful marking out and relying solely on the chisel section to give the letter stems their finished shape is at best a very uncertain technique. An exception to this might be the 'rustic' type of nameplate where the wood has usually been sawn obliquely across the trunk or tree branch to preserve a bark-covered edge. In this case, the grain must be considered as 'end on' and a gouge is certainly the best tool to start and finish this type of lettering job with.

The type of house nameplate that the postman never forgets (mahogany).

V cut letter carving

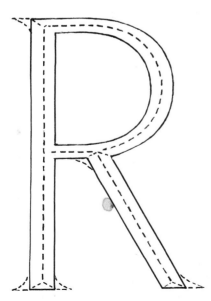

Centre the incision lines for veed lettering.

The more common method of sinking letters is considerably slower and infinitely more precise than that just described. After tracing the characters onto the wood, the outline of each letter stem and curve must be marked with a centreline. Then make a vertical cut along the centrelines to the required depth, using a gouge of suitable section to stab the curves. The next step is to vee out the letter by making chisel cuts from either side of the central incision. Start slightly inside the outline, making the chisel cuts progressively wider and deeper. When the letters are deep enough, the veeing out can be evened off by finely trimming the stems in a lengthwise direction. Curves are treated in a similar manner by using the chisel on its ground bevel.

Serifs can be added when the veeing out of the letters has been completed. Before you start adding the serifs, however, the letter ends will need to be incised at a suitable angle; the slope will depend on the depth of the letters. Use the corner of a chisel to get the right angle of incision.

The addition of serifs requires extreme care, and there is always a tendency to over-carve this detail. The removal of too much wood from the letter corners will ruin the whole effect. The corner of a freshly honed chisel must be used to gently pare off the tiniest of chips leading to the sting of the serif, which is no more than a fine incision.

The most rewarding stage when carving incised lettering is when the face of the workpiece is ready for cleaning off with glass-

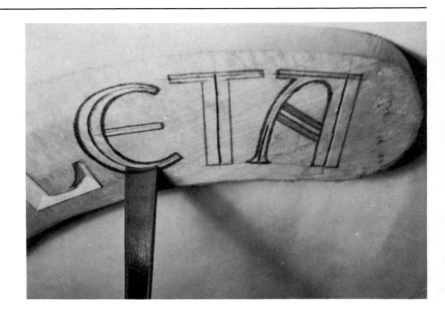

Incising the letter centres before veeing them out.

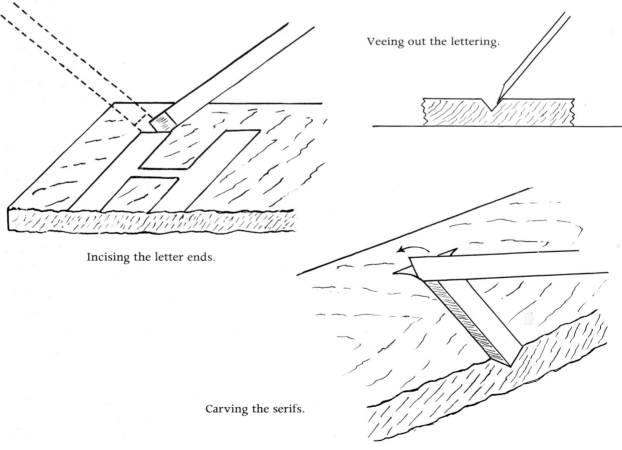

Veeing out the lettering.

Incising the letter ends.

Carving the serifs.

Trimming off the sides of the veeing.

paper, which must be wrapped around a flat block of wood. The slightly less than smooth texture of the lettering provides crisp contrast with the flawless smoothness of the surface. By lowering the surface fractionally, it is possible to correct any slight deviations in the stem widths. This manoeuvre will not, of course, help if the veed centres require straightening. In that case a three-cornered riffler file will be needed to rub straight any wavering of the lower centrelines.

Flat lettering

Flat-bottomed letters with vertical sides are rather more tricky to sink. This type of letter does not have the advantage of any real depth to provide clarity, so sharp corners are essential to a clear outline. The corners should be marked out with a fine point, leaving no margin for error during the initial incising of the outlines. Start emptying the outlines by sloping off the waste from the stem centres to meet the outline incision. This will leave a raised ridge of waste in the centre of the letters, which in turn can be removed by using a chisel worked on its ground bevel. It is usually necessary to level off the 'floor' of the letters with a flat curved riffler file. Sometimes the internal outline will lend itself to being frosted with a matting punch, which will provide greater definition. As described above, the face of the board can be glass-papered to a smooth finish.

Raised lettering

It is more common to sink letters than to raise them, but there is no reason why raised lettering should not be equally attractive and functional. A dropped background also permits the use of a

Preliminary groundwork for raising a letter (left) and sinking a letter (right).

matting punch for greater clarity, which is particularly useful when the lettering is carved on a curved surface. There may, however, be the odd occasion when raised lettering is not entirely practical; for instance, if the centre of a panel is to be inscribed, the background needs to be contained within a frame. The frame may distract the eye from the inscription or produce a less attractive effect than sunken lettering would do.

Here the technique requires that the chisel be inclined away from the letter edge, on the waste side of the line. Take care when chiselling the waste – light pressure should be used to avoid bursting the short grain features of the letters. The waste must be removed from immediately around the letters by sloping it off towards the letter stems. A spoon bit chisel can then work more freely away from the letters to dispose of the larger areas of background. Smooth unblemished ground work is not essential; a uniform chip effect from the chisel can enhance the finished effect, though of course this will depend on the style and context of the lettering.

Any of the foregoing techniques will work equally well with numerals. But when a figure or combination of figures require prominence, it may be best to profile rather than carve the numerals from a solid face. Decorative work will have to be in keeping with the way in which the numerals will be used. Inevitably, profiled numerals will not be very robust, but gluing them to the base board with paper in between should give adequate security.

Power tool lettering

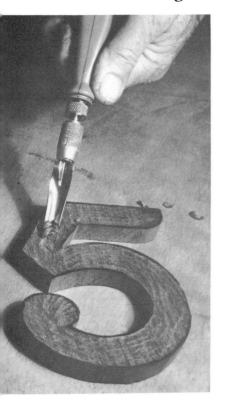

At this point, we can mention a radically different method of letter cutting. It is possible to use an electrically-powered machine, called the Burgess engraver, to drive the chisel tip. Clearly, this makes carving a lot less effort. The force will not be as powerful as the ordinary mallet and chisel, but it is worth considering as an optional extra for the tool kit.

The machine has interchangeable cutting tips for wood, and is also equipped with points for engraving metal and plastic. There are two choices of speed, controllable by switch, and a fine adjustment control of the cutting stroke. Waste removal is not as fast as when a mallet and chisel are used, but providing the machine is allowed to work to its own capacity, the result is indistinguishable from normal practice. It goes without saying, of course, that the cutting tips must all be kept properly honed.

Another more expensive machine tool that may be used for letter cutting is the vertical router, which has a rotary cutting action. A high speed cutting bit is entered into the surface of the wood at a pre-determined depth, and moved around freehand to mill out grooving to the required width. Being of robust construction, its manoeuvrability on small work is rather limited.

Concaving the surface of a numeral with a gouge tip fitted into an electric engraving machine.

7 Carving in the round

Figure carving

Sculpturally, carving 'in the round' has more creative appeal than relief work. Free from the limitations of depth, any carver whose interest in the craft is purely artistic can enjoy complete freedom of three-dimensional expression. Speaking practically, carving 'in the round' also involves more physical effort, at least during the roughing out stages, and greater variation in chisel technique, due to the changes in working positions necessary for this kind of modelling.

Grain direction will dictate how far any feature can be modelled with a chisel, and the problem also arises when the feature is hard to get at – the confined inside surface of an arm or leg, for instance. Limbs play an important part in suggesting movement in any composition, human or animal. You can, of course, simplify matters by concealing the arms and legs with drapes, or, with some animals, with fur. But as you progress you will find this subterfuge unsatisfactory.

No other subject is quite as adaptable as the human figure, and providing the basic proportions are approximately correct, it is possible to gain a good effect without anatomical perfection. Nevertheless, the beginner will certainly benefit by first carving one or two unclothed figures – in fact, if the human skeleton were rather more beautiful, that would be the thing to start with. In time, you will know instinctively when the proportional roughing out is ready for further development.

There are many attitudes which provide interesting ideas for carving; I think that all action models are best portrayed with a stylized physique. A plain smooth figure can be carved from any species of wood. With character figures, however, detail must be accentuated, and a timber that has a close knit grain texture is essential. Children and old people make excellent subjects.

Every carver should cultivate an eye for the possibilities afforded by tree branch formations. They often provide an interesting basis for carving the female form, and malformation of tree growth can also offer scope for a model that would otherwise prove impossible to handle.

Carved figures of mother and child, by Peter Etheredge (oak).

A collection of carvings 'in the round'. Above left: a pair of wrestlers by a 15 year old secondary school student; above right: a character study which relies on detail for effect; below left: an ornamental figure with distinctive grain formation; below right: a piece of tree branch (sycamore) which required little adjustment to change into a figure.

50   The figure of an injured man, carved by a North American Indian.

Carving of two figures, from the Gold Coast/ Belgian Congo.

Outline planning

Unless the figure is standing rigidly to attention, profile waste is unavoidable. A horizontally outstretched arm will leave a block of waste underneath it. If you do not want to do a great deal of profiling, an alternative is to glue on protrusions before profiling the outline. Providing the wood is a perfect match, this arrangement is quite satisfactory. Gluing of a more elaborate nature may prove necessary if you have to make up the required thickness. In that case you will need to plane the surfaces to be glued very carefully. To ensure that both faces are perfectly flat give one a dusting with chalk: it will show up any high spots when rubbed against its opposite number. Immediately the glue has been applied both pieces must be G cramped together and left to dry for at least 24 hours. If the facing off has been done properly, the glue line will be barely distinguishable.

Medium hardwood is most suitable when outstretched limbs must be cut from the one block of stuff. Mahogany of sufficient bulk can usually be obtained if you have to carve protruding outlines from a single piece of wood.

Whatever the subject, the initial working outline for a model in the round should be such that it will continue to be informative when any or all surface illustration has been carved off. Before tracing on the subject, its position in relation to the grain direction must be considered. Generally, with figures, the model length will run with the grain, though this will not necessarily mean that every feature will be strong or easy to carve.

A design for an adjustable book stand.

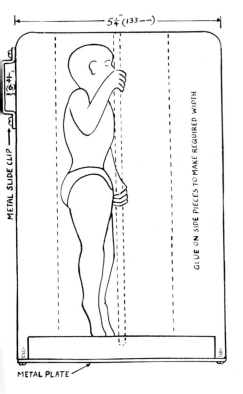

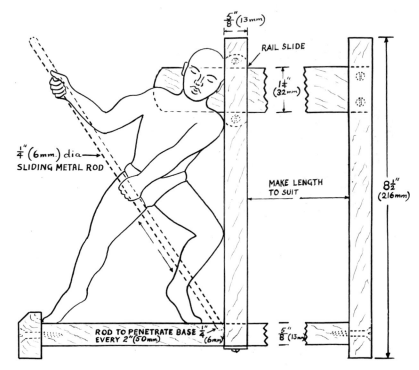

The enclosed apertures are cleaned out from the outline.

After the outline has been profiled (see chapter 3 for the method) there may be difficulties in handling the trimming-off stage if there are surface features that require relieving. The anchoring points for G cramps must be trustworthy; it is courting disaster to use a short-grained limb for this purpose. If the surface area is too sparse for G cramps to be used, the job should be screwed on a base board and worked in a similar manner as a relief carving would be. The screws should be positioned to enter what will be the reverse waste on the model. This problem can be avoided if the figure is designed complete with a base or with a similar solid wood append-age, such as a book end. If this is the case, the outline can be cramped solidly down on the work top.

Roughing out and rounding off

It is not easy to control the chisel during the roughing out stage when the surface of the figure is uneven. If the gouge requires more than usual push, a little gentle assistance with a mallet will reduce the risk of slipping under or over a starting edge. When the bulk of the waste has been removed from the front of the model it can be turned over for similar treatment; the rear contours can be drawn on the side of the model. Both the front and rear shape may be marked on before carving commences, but over-ambitious marking out can often lead to an impossibly difficult outline.

Without a flat surface on the wood it will be more difficult to cramp it down securely. However, that may be turned to advantage. If the model is held in the vice it may be possible to remove the bulk of the waste by sawing. This will reduce heavy chisel work to a minimum.

Further shaping must be more restrained. The figure should retain its square state until the proportioning has been finalised from every angle. Commence the rounding off with a straight chisel; this stage of the work must be unhurried and you should not concentrate too much on any particular feature. At this stage, depending on the size of the model, it may be possible and more convenient, to rest the model against the bench top without fixing it securely, to permit constant change of position. The extremities, head, hands and feet can be left in a rough state until all adjustment to the overall shape has been completed.

Carving the detail

Round and half round files are invaluable for achieving the more subtle curves. Muscles should be carved when you have a clear picture of where they should be on the body.

Detailing of the face, hands and feet can start when their basic shape has been modelled. As there is little margin for error, this is one case where detail must be clearly defined with a sharp pencil point. The safest technique for carving small features is to ensure that every chipping is incised before you attempt to remove it. This type of delicate incision can be done with the point of a skew chisel, waste being lifted out from one or both sides of the incision. Figures generally look more acceptable with a smooth finish, and glass-papering round the limbs will clean off inaccessible parts.

Clothed figures demand special treatment. A loose fitting gown

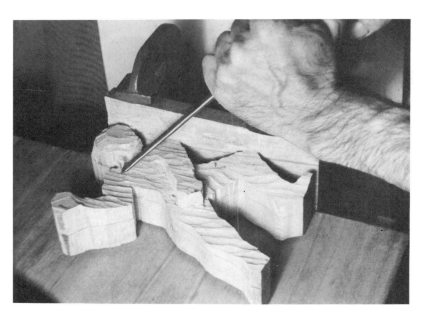

Relieving the surface features.

The finished model.

will involve careful gouge work to create a draping effect. With tight-fitting clothes which show sharp creases at bent limb joints, the required effect can be gained by notching with a straight chisel. Clothes can impart a sense of time and character to a figure subject; if the bones of the model are of little interest, research into fashion can often lead to an authenticity which will do much to compensate for physical shortcomings.

Carving animals

Animals always provide interesting subjects, and the most ordinary creatures somehow acquire fresh originality when created in wood. Different breeds of dog, cat and so on offer further scope for expression. A cat can be depicted as a Manx, Siamese, Cheshire or 'wild' cat with arched back and upright tail. You can enlarge the proportions to carve jungle big cats. It would be wrong to single out any particular animal as being more suitable than others to carve, for the most unlikely creatures can often make absorbing subjects.

For the moment, discussion will be confined to mammals with a 'leg in each corner' though I hesitate to think how many animals fit this description. For our purpose, all animals have one thing in common, and that is that they need to be carved in sufficiently strong wood. Any of the African mahoganies fall within this category, and their reddish-brown colouring make them especially suitable for many fur-covered animals. Teak, walnut, sycamore and plane are other hardwoods that withstand deep separation of the grain structure, and which are therefore suitable for representing fur.

The procedure for carving any animal with four feet on the ground is fairly constant irrespective of size and species. Assuming the animal is standing four square, the grain direction must run with the legs. Therefore, the initial drawing will be traced on to fit, nose to tail, within the width of the wood. The second consideration is whether a base will be part of the model's structure or will be added on as a separate component on completion, though if the model is reasonably stable, a base may not be necessary.

The inclusion of a base will trap the waste wood between the legs, and if this happens the waste must be drilled out from both a sideways and end-on position. Without a base, straight saw cuts down each side of the legs can be linked by drilling to release the waste. The remainder of the profiling can be handled by sawing or link drilling with the usual follow up with chisel and file to bring the outline to more precise lines. The tapering off of the head and

The roughly hewn out shape of a horse, which is shown here in its finished form. The stance of this model makes inclusion of a base optional (Burmese teak).

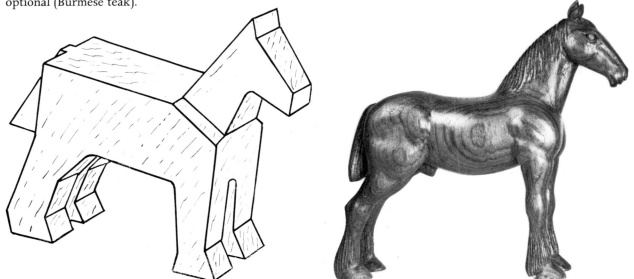

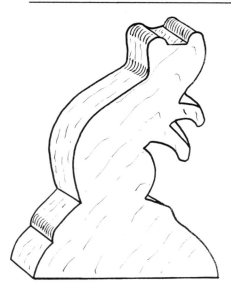

neck will involve further waste removal; a wedge-shaped piece should be sawn off each side of these features.

Where possible, the frontal shape of a feature should be drawn on the square cut outline to assist with the shaping. Under no circumstances must the ears be separated until the general proportioning is completed. Soft furry animals are not so exacting to model as the more angular species, as their shape develops gradually during the process of rounding off. A couple of straight chisels and a file will take any subject to a state of near completion.

Animals' tails deserve special mention. Unless this feature figures prominently in the identity of the species, carving the tail is likely to be an irritating but essential task during the parting of the hind legs. Short, thin curly tails can be simply relieved on the hind quarters with a slight amount of undercutting to suggest separation. Long luxurious tails deserve the full 'stand off' treatment, though whenever possible they should swirl to a convenient anchoring point for greater strength.

If the animal looks effective without fur, then it is probably best not to suggest it. Smooth, short haired animals respond well to a high degree of finishing. If, on the other hand, the species is well known for its abundance of fur, it can be shown by intermittent partings in the coat. The corner of a straight chisel or a V parting tool will produce the required effect.

We usually see a stoat on its hind legs, so a base is needed for this design.

A V parting tool can be used to suggest fur.

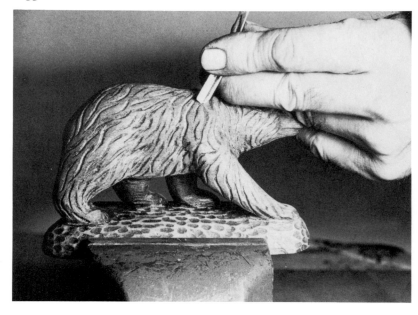

A seal, carved from a section of branch, by a 15 year old.

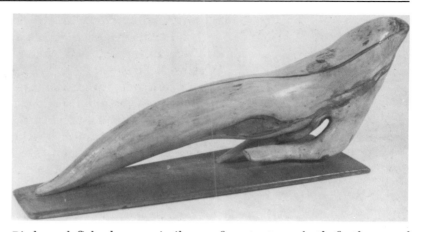

Birds and fish

Birds and fish share a similar surface texture, both feathers and scales requiring an almost identical carving technique. However, wings are carved differently from fins; the wings are part of the body of the bird when folded, and carving is mainly confined to showing the principle flight feathers. Birds' legs and claws are more of a problem, but to make things easier the claws can be incorporated into an appropriate design (suggestive of foliage, perhaps). Apart from ensuring that the legs benefit from the grain strength and thickening them slightly, there is not much else other than artificial reinforcement that you can do to increase their strength. Birds of prey are less difficult since their legs are well feathered, and their talons more substantial than those of other birds.

The most popular positions for a bird to be carved in are those of taking off or landing. In either case the wings are outspread and the claws are attached to the ground. Carved from a single piece of wood, both postures will involve a period of prolonged waste removal. The shaping should start with the underside of the wing spread, the upper curvature being roughed out with a saw and pared off to match the sweep of the underside.

A less wasteful method is to construct the bird from partly pre-shaped pieces, legs and wings being added to the body. Whereas the legs can be a straightforward push fit into the body, or, with the feathered variety, can be stub dowelled, affixing the wings is a more critical operation. Here the roots or thick ends of the wings must be raised from the body to form a natural joint. The wings are then glued in position and carefully pared off to flow into the roots. After the feathers have been carved on the wing surface, it will be very difficult to detect the join.

Producing a feathered effect is extremely simple; a gouge of suitable size and section is used to stab the feather ends, which are then relieved in a downward direction before the next line of feathers is registered with the gouge. Every alternate line is staggered to bring the half circles between the points of the preceding line. Full length flight feathers must be incised with a straight chisel, and relieved in a downwards direction to show the feather ridge.

Fish are not the most inspiring creatures to carve for they offer little opportunity for original presentation. Also, the most straightforward fish will prove almost as slippery to hold as the real thing. The most practical method of handling this shape is to glue two pieces of wood together lightly to make up the required body thickness. After profiling, the halves are separated and their surface made ready for marking on the carving detail. Thereafter, each workpiece can be secured in the same way as a relief carving. Before the scales can be carved (a technique which is precisely the same as feather cutting), the fins will have to be relieved. Although the size, shape and position of the fins are peculiar to every species of fish, their treatment is fairly constant. Folded flat against the body, a fin looks most effective when lightly relieved with slight undercutting of its outline.

Gouge work dominates this type of subject; the head and in certain instances the fins, will require the attention of this tool. Finely cut grooves will be necessary to cope with the surface details. When both halves of the fish have been carved they can be permanently glued together and drilled for a single stem mounting on a base of suitable shape.

Smooth skinned fish, usually of the big game variety, do not usually need to be carved in two halves. With these fish, the emphasis is on speed, strength and streamlining. Without surface detail to contend with, the body shape and heavy fins can with-

Fish, carved in oak, mounted on a metal stem.

stand fairly robust handling as a one-piece carving. Go for an action outline – it will look effective and compensate for lack of detailed work.

Apart from marking and cutting out the outline, the only other major operation is rounding off. This can be accomplished by holding the job in the vice while the corners are roughed off with a chisel. The fins of deep sea predators are not so delicately hinged as those of less lethal fish, and the point where they join the body should be blended in smoothly. Files and glass-paper will achieve the surface smoothness necessary to show off the grain to its best advantage, and the effect can be further enhanced by carefully glazing the model with a surface coating.

A woodcarver can pick and choose from nature with the safe assurance that whatever the subject, it will provide a better understanding of his medium. However, he should resist the temptation to concentrate on creatures that look cute, cuddly or noble – they do not offer the best way to gain experience and tend to become tedious. Every now and again, it can prove most refreshing to model an unusual animal. A quick browse through the A to Z of animals will always unearth some neglected creature worthy of closer examination.

Animal projection carving

Carving animals from block-shaped timber can provide hours of pleasure. There is, however, another method of modelling four-legged animals which is more suitable if a thick piece of timber is not available. This technique is a combination of 'in the round' and heavy relief carving which employs perspective as a substitute for

This animal is not as robust as it looks . . .

. . . the overhead view shows
how to taper the rhino's body
and get maximum effect out of
a narrow piece of wood.

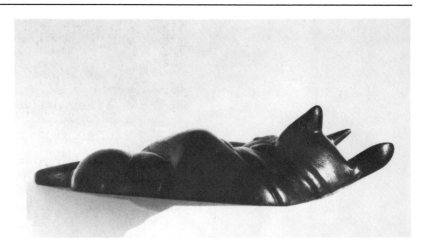

timber thickness. To gain the right effect, the wood must be wedge-
shaped to start with, its top edge also being sloped off towards the
rear. Some slight abnormality of the outline drawing will be
necessary, for it will have to depict a three-quarter viewpoint
which is always more confusing to draw than to carve. An attached
base should be included in the layout.

For the most part, the far side of this type of model will remain
perfectly flat until the front has been fully modelled. This conveniently gives you two working positions, one with the workpiece
flat against the bench top, the other with it held vertically in the
vice. Generally, no more than the nose of the animal attains a fully
rounded state, this being quite sufficient to convey the right
impression. A wedge-shaped piece of the same species of wood
should be glued to the reverse side of the base to stabilise it.

8 Heads

Beginners are often afraid of carving the human face, although it is a subject with which they are extremely familiar. Eventually, though, it will be unavoidable – perhaps a figure carving will mean that there must be some small attempt at carving human expression. Carving a face in keeping with the size of the figure is not easy to do – and if the result is disappointing, it is easy not to want to try again. This is a pity, for faces always make interesting models and carving faces is one of the oldest traditions of the craft.

Proportioning the head

A face without a head becomes a mask, and this simple fact is often overlooked because of a natural impatience to start carving the interesting bit of the job. If you can imagine it, a head should conform to the shape of one-and-a-half eggs, with half an egg attached at a right-angle to the wide end of the whole egg. Irrespective of whether the subject is bald or has hair, this shape should be marked on the wood to assess the overall proportions. A fair margin of space must surround this basic layout to accommodate the features.

If the model is started from a round portion of tree, two flat sides will have to be planed so that the design can be marked out. When using wood which has been planed all round, the best sectional shape to start with is square. The shoulders must be roughed out too, for apart from forming a natural base for the model, they will also provide a solid platform for holding the job down with a carver's screw, or for gripping in the vice.

No attempt should be made to profile the features during the roughing out stage. The bulk of the waste can be removed with a panel saw and after that with a gouge and mallet. When the head has been chipped off to an even roundness, use a shaper file to make the surface smoother. Then, mark two centre lines, down and across the ovoid shape. The vertical line will help you centre the nose and lips and the line across the face will mark the position of the eyes in relation to the head length.

In common with all relief work, it would be a waste of time to draw in the features until the highest point has been raised. With head carving, the nose and ears must be given priority (assuming the latter are not obscured by hair). Start carving the nose with

Roughing out the shape of a head.

shallow saw cuts to register the length. Relieving the tip and sloping off the nose will necessarily flatten off the upper and lower areas of the face, and this levelling off is further accentuated when the nose sides are cut down and relieved. When a fairly substantial wedge-shaped protrusion has been raised, the forehead can be sloped off and the whole rounded off again.

Shaping the features

The shaping of the features must commence with the nose. The three-dimensional aspect of the nose can prove exasperatingly difficult to capture; unless the sides are sloped into the face properly, it will look stuck on. Using a gouge of suitable size should make it look more natural and will also shape the hollows of the nostrils. Keep looking in the mirror when carving the nostrils – it will help you to be accurate.

Before the eyes are carved, the face width must be decided. If there is hair or if the subject is wearing anything that will frame the face, then this must be set back to give a clear picture of the available space; remember that, while the nose and lips can be narrowed or shortened, the eyes once carved cannot be adjusted. A gouge will rough out the eye socket depressions and raise sufficient flesh for modelling the lips. At this stage the contours of the face should be forming; the neck section should also become reduced and rounded along with the rest of the face.

The carving of the nostrils in relation to the lips can be quite tricky. Changing over to a straight chisel for undercutting the nostrils requires a radical change of technique after the subtle use of the gouge to blend the bridge into the nostrils. The modelling is further complicated by the nostril division, which must slope into the curve of the lip. This detail is a key factor in the shaping of the lips, for the bow of the upper lip is a concave continuation of the nostril division. Successful lips must swell outwards naturally; a sharp outline will destroy this effect. An indirect approach with a small gouge will allow you to develop the outer shape gradually until the stage is reached when their centre parting can be cut. Generally, the lower lip is less wide, less protruberant and fuller

Ready for marking out the features.

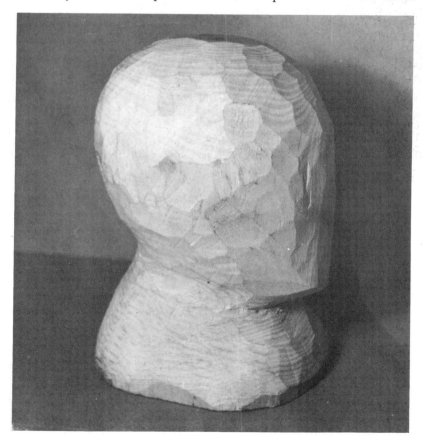

The detailed modelling is now put
in.

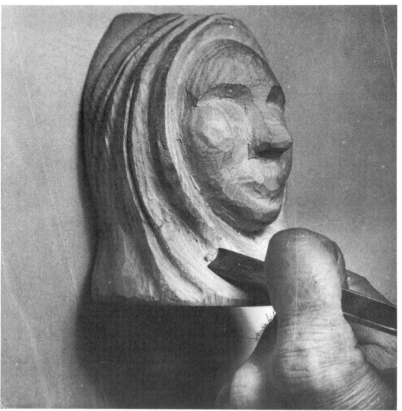

The finished model.

than the upper lip. With this in mind, the centre parting can be lightly incised before it is developed into a groove, which is then softened to suggest the roundness of the upper and lower lips. The mouth of a carved face is the only feature that is quick to show feeling and a slight hardness of the centre parting or turning up of the corners can alter the whole personality of the model.

The outline of the eyes is also difficult to clarify; the problem with the eyeball is how to suggest detail on what should really be a smooth surface. But the beginner's immediate difficulty is to put them in the right place, which is on the centre line running across the face. Fairly generous ovals must be raised and trimmed off to make the correct outline. There should be one eye's length separating both of them. The features need to be balanced with each other during this stage, and the bridge of the nose may require some adjustment to accommodate the eyes. Relieving the eyelids calls for very gentle chisel treatment, as the wood is more inclined to part on the weaker side of the incision. The upper lid should start and finish from corner to corner, the lower lid terminating at each end on a slightly lower level. Having incised the lids, the smallest of chippings must be removed, taking extreme care not to over-cut into the fine edges being relieved.

The carver can only depict the irises as raised or sunken circles. Although either method is suitable for any type of face, I think the beginner would be more successful relieving the circles for his

Expressionistic heads, carved by secondary school students.

65

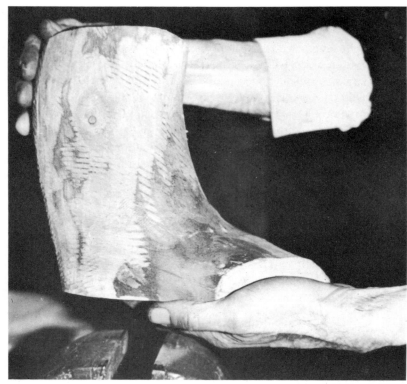

A piece of tree that would give any carver a 'head start'.

The finished head still leans with the wind which shaped the tree.

A cheerful old man, carved in ash.

first attempt. In fact, the irises are not complete circles, but are cut off top and bottom by the eyelids. When relieving this coloured area of the eye, it is important that the raised detail has a sharp unbroken edge, otherwise the effect will be lost through lack of clear cut definition.

The depth of the sunken area should be just enough to create a shadow when viewed from an angle. This effect will be enhanced by indenting the pupil. A sharp point will register the pupil, which is then lightly touched with a revolving drill point before being punched with a round-ended background tool.

It is also possible to carve the eyes with closed lids, which is especially useful for small work when the facial detail is indistinct. Here a cleanly cut ridge is all that is necessary, though the curvature of the eyeball must be shown beneath the closed lid.

Treatment of the hair often depends on the age of the subject. Young people's hair can often be left as a loose hanging mass; for a balding head, a V-parting tool will groove out just enough strands to create the right impression.

Aged craggy features are particularly enjoyable to carve and are not so demanding as a smooth unwrinkled complexion. Wrinkles can be etched in with a V-parting tool or cut to varying degrees of width and depth with a straight chisel. If you wish to give the subject hollow cheeks a gouge will pare out the necessary amount of wood, but be careful not to overdo the effect.

9 Carving small

However small an article, you can still gain a great deal of useful experience and enjoyment while carving it. Scraps of stuff that would be thrown away by a conventional woodworker can often be effectively employed by a carver. You can try chess sets, pipes, designs for pendants, to mention just a few ideas. But although an article may be small, this does not mean that it should be undertaken lightly. When tried and trusted methods of holding a small workpiece cannot be employed or are abandoned at a very early stage, shelve the job until you are absolutely certain you can manage it.

You can afford to be choosy over timber when there is not much of it to buy; moreover, small useful objects are often hollow, or are made to contain something. A cavity in any shape or form will mean that much of the wood's strength is taken away when the model is worked from a solid piece of stuff. I use the word cavity rather than hole, for the latter word may give the idea that every internal space ought to be smooth and circular. This can sometimes be true, as for instance when a hole is bored to accomodate a small clock mechanism. But more often than not, circular holes are stopped to provide a bottom or floor to the article, which means that making a hole is a job which demands considerable care and attention.

There are different kinds of cavity, of course; there is the deep slot shape such as might be needed if you wish to insert a table lighter ignition pack, or there is the shape required if you want to make a piggy bank, when you would need to carve two bowl-shaped halves.

One inflexible rule when carving a model that requires a cavity is that any boring or chiselling out must be completed before the external shaping is begun. A large circular space or slot can be started by link drilling, which will honeycomb the waste, but if only one side of the wood is pierced, the waste will have to be weakened further by vertical separation with a chisel. Eventually, the splinters break off at their roots and there should be sufficient space for cleaning off the walls of the cavity. Depending on how much space there is, the bottom of a cavity can be tidied up with a spoon bit chisel or cleaned off with a stiff scraper.

Having had its strength removed internally, the workpiece cannot be squeezed in a vice until the space is filled with temporary packing. A more artful method of gripping a small model is to plan the design so that it includes a short stub of waste wood as part of the outline. To be trustworthy, this protrusion must be placed so as to run with the grain. When the work has progressed to a less energetic stage of chiselling, the waste can be removed.

Obviously, small work will to some extent require small tools.

Supreme examples of the woodcarver's art – Japanese netsuke, from the 18th and 19th centuries.

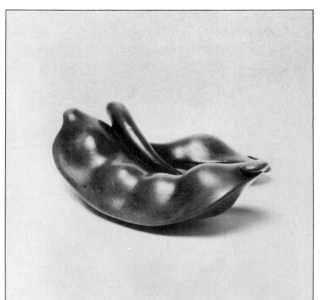

Woodcarving

A piggy bank, carved from two halves (obeche).

A tiny scrap of oak was used for this brooch.

A sprightly mahogany jester surmounts a small clock.

Chisels can be used for work of wide-ranging sizes, but files are not so accommodating. This is especially true of the round and half round variety, and small inside curvatures are very difficult to finish without a file to suit the job. Exceptionally fine detail may benefit from the attention of needle files. As the name suggests, this type of file is extremely fine in shape and cut, terminating in a point that is every bit as sharp as a needle. They are manufactured in a variety of shapes and are usually purchased as a set in a protective wallet.

Carving jewellery

Small tools are certainly essential for the carving of brooches and pendants. A really close-knit hardwood is more likely to survive the test of time than timber that is easy to carve; beech and sycamore are just two perennially obtainable species.

With small work, your fingers and the chisel edge are bound to be close together – so, for safety's sake, it is wise to glue the model down to a piece of board after it has been profiled with a coping saw. All the surface detail can then be carved with the board cramped to the work top, and the model need only be released for finishing off with files and glass-paper.

A hole for the cord or chain should be designed as part of a pendant rather than simply drilled as an afterthought. Modern glue has simplified the fixing of brooch pins. Many carvers vary their effects by including inlays of polished brass and perspex in the design, and coloured glass and pieces of polished stone may be used too. Generally, a hard durable varnish type of finish looks perfectly acceptable on carved jewellery.

10 Bowls and dishes

Although it may not appear so at first, digging out the interior of a bowl or dish is a very relaxing occupation and because of the shape of the depression and the type of tool used it is difficult to spoil the work through lack of skill or through impatience. Virtually any species of wood will be suitable for carving bowls provided that it is of sufficient width. The depth of a modern fruit bowl is well within the capacity of medium sized gouges and only a couple of these tools are necessary to handle the functional part of the job. Trinket trays, ash trays and other small receptacles are worked in basically the same way, with allowance made for their size.

If the intention is to carve a circular receptacle, the workpiece must remain square for convenience of holding until the interior

Start digging out the interior with a gouge.

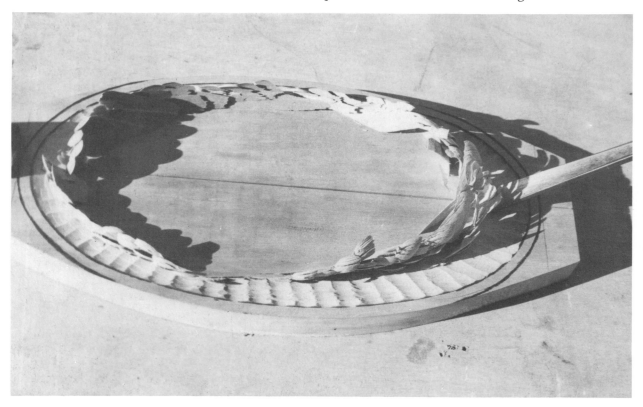

has been completed. The shape will suggest the best method of securing the work. An oval dish, after being roughed off with a saw, will require a G cramp to hold down one end, while the front edge can be prevented from moving forwards with a bench stop. A similar set up is possible with a round bowl, though here the G cramp will be positioned on a rear corner of the yet unshaped piece of plank. The thickness of wood can range from 32 mm ($1\frac{1}{4}$ in.) to 45 mm ($1\frac{3}{4}$ in.) for a bowl, while a dish can be as slender as 22 mm ($\frac{7}{8}$ in.). After marking the outer shape, the inside perimeter can be carefully drawn in to determine the thickness of the bowl's edge. This depends on the overall size, but must not be much less than 6 mm ($\frac{1}{4}$ in.).

Removal of the centre waste must start with a straight gouge positioned at a fairly gentle angle on the drawn-in perimeter of the bowl. With assistance from a mallet, the gouge should be worked around the inside edge at a constant cutting force. A consistent approach will help the shape to take form surely. Then the centre area of waste can be cleared before you start to work the gouge round again. This time, the gouge cuts are started slightly below the bowl edge. You will find that the gouge shows a natural inclination to terminate its chip when used at a steeper angle on the

The shape is here being finalised, ready for glass papering.

Careful glass papering brings the interior to a flawless finish.

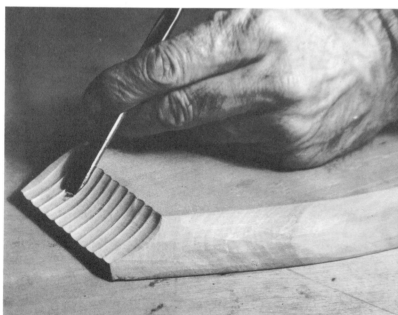

Dish handles may be given 'non-slip' finger grips.

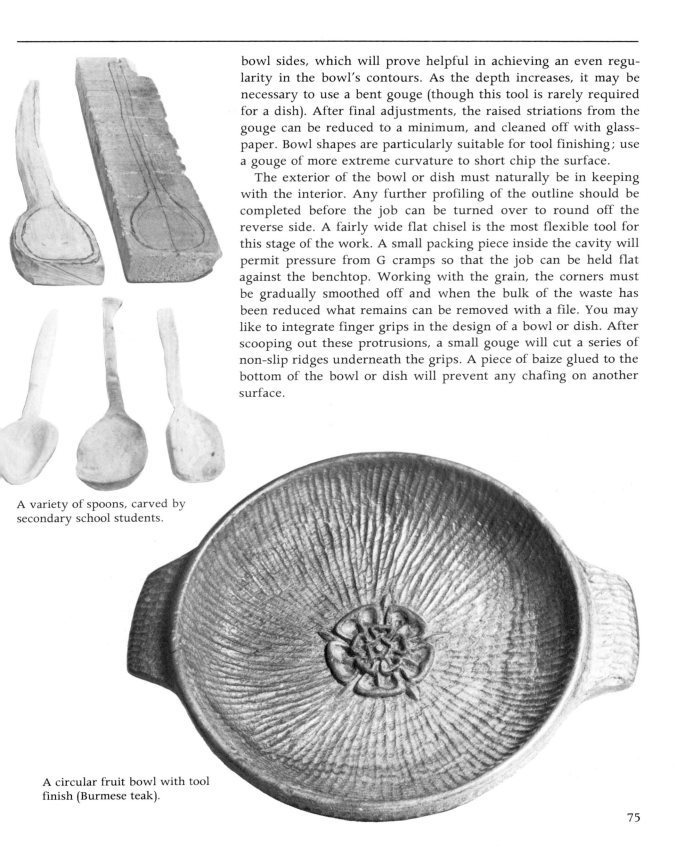

bowl sides, which will prove helpful in achieving an even regularity in the bowl's contours. As the depth increases, it may be necessary to use a bent gouge (though this tool is rarely required for a dish). After final adjustments, the raised striations from the gouge can be reduced to a minimum, and cleaned off with glasspaper. Bowl shapes are particularly suitable for tool finishing; use a gouge of more extreme curvature to short chip the surface.

The exterior of the bowl or dish must naturally be in keeping with the interior. Any further profiling of the outline should be completed before the job can be turned over to round off the reverse side. A fairly wide flat chisel is the most flexible tool for this stage of the work. A small packing piece inside the cavity will permit pressure from G cramps so that the job can be held flat against the benchtop. Working with the grain, the corners must be gradually smoothed off and when the bulk of the waste has been reduced what remains can be removed with a file. You may like to integrate finger grips in the design of a bowl or dish. After scooping out these protrusions, a small gouge will cut a series of non-slip ridges underneath the grips. A piece of baize glued to the bottom of the bowl or dish will prevent any chafing on another surface.

A variety of spoons, carved by secondary school students.

A circular fruit bowl with tool finish (Burmese teak).

11 Carving for casting

The average carver dislikes repeating a model; it is monotonous and rather uninspiring to retrace old ground. Often a reasonable facsimile of the original is acceptable, in a material other than wood and 'manufactured' rather than carved. This is made possible by a process nearly as old as woodcarving itself. A model (known as a pattern in this process) is carved from which a mould is taken, and then replicas are cast from this mould.

Principles of mould making

The pattern will be tightly entombed in a hard drying mould-making substance, and this should be borne in mind when the pattern is being carved. If a pattern of suitable shape is chosen, separating the mould from the pattern should not present any difficulties. If, however, the pattern shape is not suitable, parting

From left to right: flat backed model, reverse impression, finished cast mounted on wood.

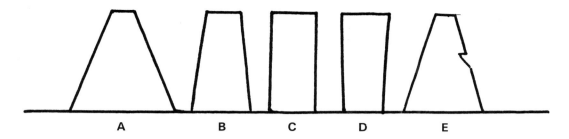

A	B	C	D	E

Some shapes are not suitable for casting. The following evaluations will help you avoid these:

A Generous taper – excellent
B Slight taper – very good
C Vertical sides – fair
D Slight adverse taper – impossible
E Small undercut – impossible

the mould from the pattern will be impossible without damage to one or the other.

The simplest shape to cast is a pyramid. Of course, not all models can be pyramid-shaped, but it is worthwhile trying to incorporate sloping sides into your design (although if a model's sides are wider at the top than at the bottom, it will be impossible to remove the mould). Every three-dimensional aspect of the pattern should be slightly wedge-shaped to make the mould easier to remove.

One problem in mould-making is an 'undercut' – any horizontal groove in the side of the pattern which runs against the direction in which the mould will be removed. Try to keep the sides of the pattern smooth, where possible.

Types of pattern

The most straightforward pattern is one carved only on one side, which can be screwed down on a baseboard and sealed off by having a minute quantity of plasticine forced between the outline and the baseboard with the point of a knife. This type of pattern is suitable for reproducing relief carvings.

If you wish to cast 'in the round' objects, you will obviously have to start with an 'in the round' pattern. Sometimes it is possible to mount this type of pattern end on to the baseboard and cast it from a vertical standpoint. Usually, though, the pattern must be carved in two halves to make a split mould, or carved as one piece and sawn down the centre. An alternative method is to glue two pieces of wood together lightly before carving, which permits easy and exact separation when the modelling is finished.

Preparing the pattern

To make sure that nothing sticks to the pattern and baseboard, they must both be coated with a hard drying surface coating such as French polish or cellulose paint. This can be done with the pattern screwed in position. After a suitable drying time, another type of coating is applied, called a releasing agent. The choice of releasing agent will depend on the type of material used to make the mould. If you intend to use dental plaster for the mould, the releasing agent can be as simple as a thin smear of wax polish on the pattern and baseboard. If more expensive resinous powder is employed, the agent must be the type supplied by the manufacturer. When the pattern is ready for casting it must be enclosed within a wooden frame, which will become part of the mould when it has hardened. The inside surface of the frame should be roughly scored for the medium to grip when the mould is ready for lifting, or the frame may slip away from the mould and leave it vulnerable to damage. The casting frame is filled by pouring the mould-making material into the frame from one corner. This must not be disturbed until the mould has thoroughly hardened. A fine wedge gently tapped between the baseboard and each corner of the frame will enable you to lift the mould off the pattern evenly. It should, of course, be remembered that whatever kind of plaster is used its residue must never be washed down the sink.

Casting from the mould

When the mould has dried out, the cavity and top surface can be painted with a hard drying enamel. Now a solid cast can be taken from the mould, the inside of which must be waxed if dental plaster is being used or coated with a specific releasing agent if resin powder is used.

There has to be a means of removing the cast once it has set, and this problem is best dealt with by submerging two mushroom-headed bolts of suitable size with wide washers on their heads during the pouring operation. A temporary bridge across the mould will hold the bolts vertical until the mould sets. A flat piece of board can then be held by the bolts against the cast and eased upwards by corner wedging. Since flat-backed reproductions are usually mounted on a wood background, the bolts can be used to fix the reproduction permanently.

Set up for removing the cast from the mould.

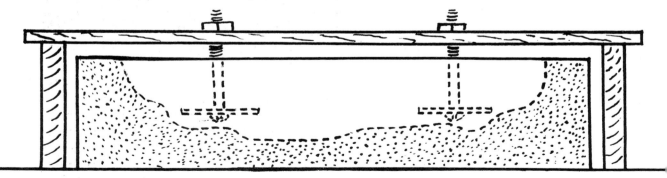

Casting 'in the round'

A large heavy model made from two pattern halves is neither desirable nor, in most cases, necessary. Provision to insert a core can be made while setting out one of the pattern halves on its baseboard. The insertion of the core will result in a hollow cavity

A model half mounted on the casting board.

down the centre of the casting. Whether this is necessary or not will depend on the size of the work.

The core can be made by tapering a piece of dowel of suitable length and diameter. After mounting the pattern, a short section of the dowelling must be positioned in the exact centre of the base of the pattern. Now casting can proceed as previously described.

Before casting the other half of the pattern, a means of aligning both cavity halves must be provided. Two round metal stubs set diagonally in the corners of the finished mould half will locate its counterpart after the second stage of casting. This can start with the removal of the frame from the existing cast and the preparation of another that will accept twice the depth of plaster or resin. Now the cavity must be filled with plasticine and the second half of the pattern positioned precisely over the outline, with the core

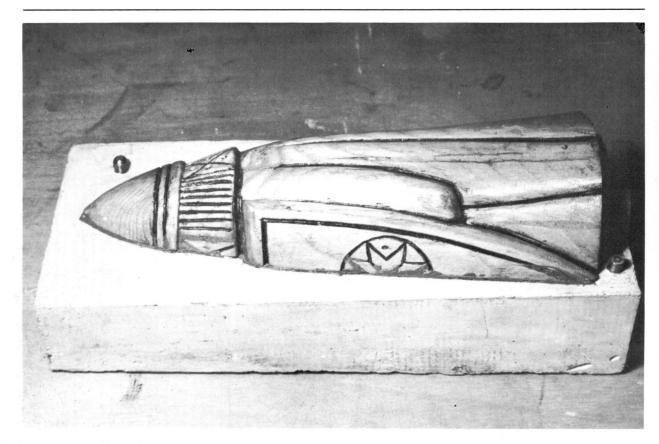

The two model halves mated, ready for casting as one.

marker placed accordingly. After treating the inside face of the frame with wax or releasing agent it can be filled and left to set.

When the frame has been completely removed, the mould halves can be parted with wedges. The second pattern half can be extracted from its cast by screwing a piece of board against the back of the flush fitting pattern, and wedging up the corners of the casting. When both halves of the mould have been suitably treated with releasing agent, they can be held together lightly with a G cramp.

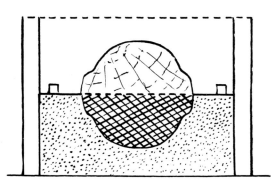

The second pattern in position, ready for casting.

The mould with the core in position. The internal cavity has been filled, and the two halves of the mould are G cramped together.

Immediately the cavity has been filled through the core opening, the core must be inserted. It will displace a certain amount of filling, but overspill is preferable to a short filled cavity. There should be little difficulty in splitting the mould; usually one of the cavity halves will be released instantly, leaving the other still attached to the reproduction. Light tapping on the back of the mould will help it on its way.

A very slight loss of definition is inevitable, but this can be put back where required by careful hand shaping with a sharp (not

The finished model, with the two halves on either side of it.

cutting) edge. Another unavoidable leftover from the casting process is a faint ridge where the mould halves were joined together. This is quickly scraped off.

Plaster can be drilled, chiselled and glass-papered, painted, stained and varnished. A thoroughly dry cast and adequate under-coating are the main essentials for a good finish. Although the end product will lack the richness of wood grain, it will always retain the character of the carved master pattern.

12 Edge carving

Ornate cabinet carving is not very common nowadays; it is usually not in keeping with modern decor and the right kind of timber is often too expensive for the average craftsman to buy. But light carving of the wood's edge can be interesting work to do, and it looks attractive.

Much modern furniture is made from laminated boards, where the edge is unsuitable for carving. If, however, the grain is more than skin deep, the edge can be embellished successfully. It is long and repetitious work, though, and it is worth experimenting on a short length of wood before embarking on the real thing. In this way you will find how best to tackle the job and what tools are necessary.

If you are making furniture, it is most convenient to carve an edge before the article of furniture is put together. A large structure such as a table top can be held by G cramps against the work bench legs. A wide, thin panel may require additional support when being held in the vice by sandwiching between two extra boards. At no time should you hold a subject while attempting to carve its edge.

Edge corner patterns

Simple notching of the edge corner may suit small pieces of furniture. It is important that the notches should be uniform. Mark a depth line on the face and edge of the wood and keep to it strictly. It is important to keep the notchings equally spaced, and dividers are useful for this. Do not attempt to cut a notch with a straight chisel without first incising the centre, for this will result in a progressive splitting of the corners. After making the cut across the grain, the downward cuts from either side must be clean and decisive. A change of technique is necessary for the end grain of the wood. Here the chisel is worked from the face with its corner inclined towards the inverted apex of the notch.

Another variation of corner carving is gouge chipping; the technique is pretty much the same as before, with one important difference. Unlike a notch, the gouge chip must look as if it has been accomplished in one uninterrupted cut. A sharp tool of well-rounded section will create the right effect. Using a gouge will also enable you to cope with the end grain without altering the action at all.

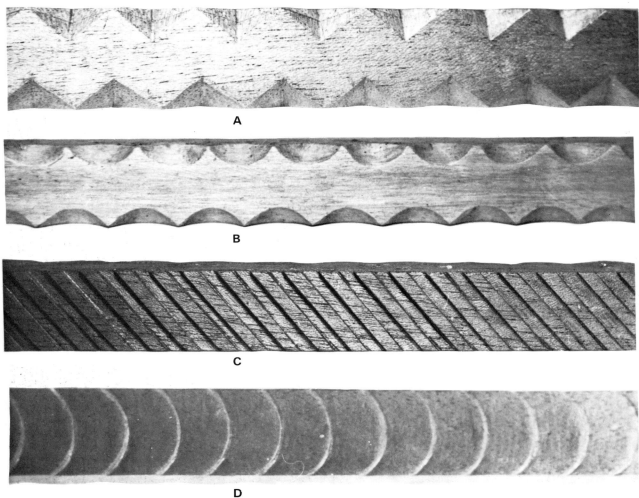

Patterns carved on the flat:
A Edge notching (straight chisel)
B Edge notching (gouge)
C Diagonal stripes (straight chisel)
D Crescent relief (gouge and straight chisel).

Patterns worked on the flat

Turning to patterns worked on the flat, the same gentle, disciplined rhythm is needed as with relief carving. Diagonal stripes are not tedious to cut if the alternating slots are of a depth just sufficient to convey a relief effect. Marking out this type of finish is as important as carving it. A piece of wood or card cut to the angle of the stripes can be used to mark them off. Use a chisel of more than adequate width and make light vertical incisions; then pare out between every alternate diagonal with a slim chisel. There should not then be a need for any further development, and in fact, a very slight roughness will enhance the top surface.

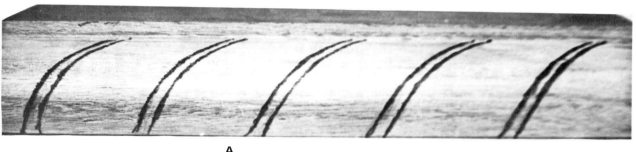

A

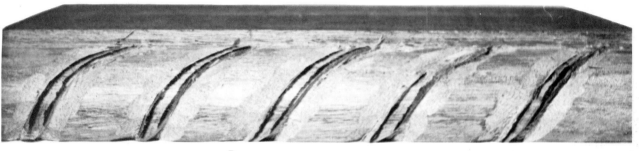

B

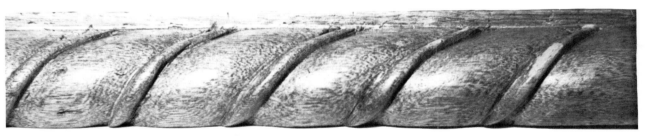

C

The main stages in carving a rope effect:
A Mark off the nosing

B The centre ridges are notched out

C The final effect, after the 'rounding over' is completed.

Using a combination of gouge and straight chisel will offer many variations of edge decoration. One quick and easy effect can be made by carving equally spaced vertical incisions with a gouge wide enough to suit the width of the edge, and then sloping off the wood preceding the convexity of each incision. If the edge width is too wide for the largest gouge size to handle, the incisions should be repeated to join at the centre of the edge.

The style of any edge finish must be in keeping with the article; as you can imagine, a substantial period table top would not be enhanced by corner chipping more suited to a cuckoo clock. A half twist or rope effect lends itself well to more classical furniture. A rebated edge is necessary to finish off the upper grooving of this design properly. The nosing of the rebate must also be rounded off before marking out.

There may be the odd occasion when a completely round length of dowel must be carved to form a grooved spiralling effect. This type of design cannot be marked out entirely freehand; adhesive tape wrapped diagonally around a circular shape will form an accurate spiral which can be followed with a pencil point. Then using a straight chisel, the lines drawn in must be incised and notched to depth which permits each division to be rounded off. The final rounding off is done with a file and glass-paper.

This kind of carving does offer scope for originality and inventiveness, though it must again be stressed that a design should be known to be practical before committing it to the wood.

13 Finishing

It is customary for the finish of woodcarving to be as close as possible to the natural state. There is no reason why a carving should be given any kind of surface coating; it is quite sufficient to leave it with a tooled or sanded finish. But there may be occasions when you feel that a particular model would look so much better for a little extra surface enhancement. Wood finishing is a highly specialised craft, and a good result cannot be wholly acquired out of a tin or bottle. More often than not, the desired finish can only be attained through effort rather than expense.

Since the majority of wood species are highly porous, any type of surface coating must be regarded as final, in the sense that once on and in the wood it will be extremely difficult to remove completely. The absorbency of wood has to be the first consideration when the question of finish comes up. What may be quite suitable for one species of timber could prove completely ineffective when applied to another grade of wood. In this respect, a pertinent factor is compatability of colouring. Any sort of coating will darken the wood to some extent (discounting bleaching treatment). Nevertheless, certain types of finish are formulated to blend unobtrusively with light or dark grained timber. Wood stain proper, however, has a more drastic colour change effect.

Wax polish

The oldest and most widely accepted method of finishing a carving is to apply a wax preparation. This is made by shredding beeswax into a tin or jar and covering it with turpentine. The receptacle is then heated by standing it in hot water or on a hot plate (under no circumstances should direct or open flame heat be used) until the wax has melted. When cool, the polish should have the consistency of soft butter. If this is not the case, it must be reheated and more wax or turpentine added. The polish is best rubbed in with a soft flannel cloth. The first couple of applications will disappear into the wood, but patience and hard rubbing will produce a hint of a shine, which is quite adequate for carvings of a traditional character. Repeated light applications over a period of time produce the best results; fewer and heavier coats will only create a tacky unpolishable build-up.

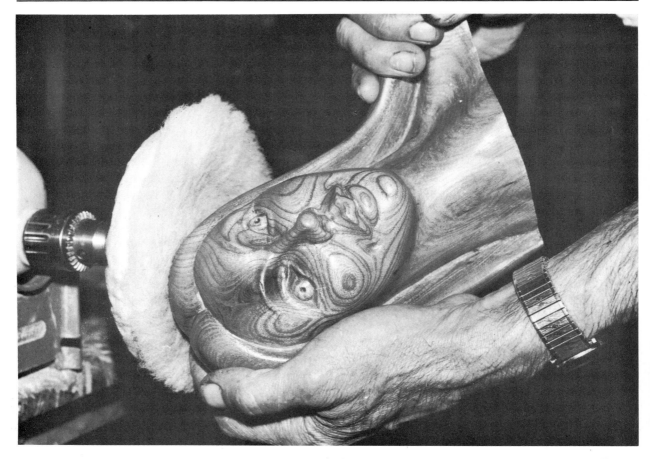

Wax polishing with a lambswool polishing pad and an electric drill.

Oil polish

Oil polish is another well-tried finish, very suitable for hardwoods such as oak, mahogany and walnut. In this case, the preparation is rather more tricky than with wax polish, and involves a greater heat source. Linseed oil is the principle constituent and because this will need to be simmered (not boiled) for a few minutes, the process is best done out of doors on a small butane gas picnic stove. When cool, one eighth of its bulk of turpentine is added. The resultant mixture penetrates quickly into the wood, and the wood will not shine until it is satiated. A fairly thick wad of flannel will hold a generous helping of polish.

French polish

French polish is a finish associated more with good class furniture than with woodcarving, but there is some carved work with which it can be used successfully. A table lamp or fruit bowl may suit the high shine which this polish gives.

To French polish a large smooth area successfully requires a great deal of practice; it is done with a 'rubber' – a wad of cloth loaded with polish. The size of most carvings rarely permits use of this technique, however, and a satisfactory application is possible using a soft-haired brush. First of all, though, the grain must be filled. There are various ways of doing this; the most straightforward method is to use a dilute mixture of the polish itself. The degree of dilution is not critical, and can be adjusted by adding a small amount of methylated spirit. Generally, two or three applications are necessary before the grain ceases to lift, and this roughness must be rubbed down in between coats with fine glass-paper. The finishing coats should not be over-brushed, or applied too thickly.

A paint brush can be used to apply French polish on a broken surface.

Varnish

Because of changes in chemical make-up, varnish today is far removed from the sticky slow-drying product of years ago. Notwithstanding this, its use should only be considered for work intended for outdoors. A varnish finish can be greatly improved if the grain is pre-filled and rubbed down before the varnish is applied. French polish is ideal for pre-filling, and it will not build up too great a thickness of surface coating, an important factor when small detail or incised lettering is likely to get clogged up through overcoating.

Stain

Because the carver is likely to use timber of high quality, he rarely has to resort to wood stain. Nevertheless there is always the odd occasion when a change of colour proves to be necessary; if ebony is unavailable, a black dye can be used to create the impression of it (though in fact, ebony is more likely to be a streaky dark brown). One cannot generalise about the way wood stains work on wood, as their behaviour is to some extent affected by the absorbent qualities of the wood being treated. Moreover, the chemical make-up varies; depending on whether a stain has an oil, spirit or water base, it will possess different spreading and drying propensities.

Caution is the keynote when applying any stain; if a brush is used, the stain may immediately penetrate too deeply or the colour will be too dense. Practise a little on scrap wood to get the feel of the stain first. Once it is dry, a top coating of French polish is usually necessary to bring out the full effect. Do not confuse wood stain with varnish stain, which must never be used on carved work.

Paint

The most direct method of adding colour is by paint, though of course this is not suitable for a great deal of work. Reproduction antique toys, however, really come to life when painted with bright enamels. The density of colouring will depend on how well the grain has been filled in, and whether it has had suitable under-coating. As an alternative, coloured dyes will give a flat, rather subdued effect, which is ideal for certain types of work.

Index